LOVE OF TH█ ███ SEA ISLANDS

THE
SALISH SEA
& ISLANDS

Quadra Is.

Cortes Is.

Savary Is.

Mitlenatch Is.

Texada Is.

Denman Is.

Jedediah Is.

Hornby Is.

Lasqueti Is.   Thormanby Is.

Gambier Is.

Bowen Is.

VANCOUVER ISLAND

SALISH SEA

Vancc

Victoria

N

Newcastle Is.

Protection Is.

Nanaimo

Gabriola Is.

Valdes Is.

Thetis Is.

Penelakut Is.

Retreat Is.

Wise Is.

Galiano Is.

SALISH SEA

Vancouver

Tsawwassen

Mayne Is.

Prevost Is.

Salt Spring Is.

Pender Is.

Saturna Is.

Tumbo Is.

VANCOUVER ISLAND

Sidney

Senanus Is.

Victoria

Orcas Is.

San Juan Is.

N

Love *of the* Salish Sea Islands

NEW ESSAYS, MEMOIRS AND POEMS BY 40 ISLAND WRITERS

*A treasury of writing celebrating the beauty, community
and importance of our archipelagos*

Mother Tongue Publishing Limited
Salt Spring Island, BC
Canada

MOTHER TONGUE PUBLISHING LIMITED
290 Fulford-Ganges Road, Salt Spring Island, B.C. V8K 2K6, Canada
www.mothertonguepublishing.com
Represented in North America by Heritage Group Distribution.

Cover, interior design and map by Mark Hand
Front Cover Painting: Southey Point, 2005, oil on canvas by Nicola Wheston
Back Cover Painting: Winter Twin Oaks, 2002, oil on canvas by Nicola Wheston
Interior title page watercolours: Adobe Stock
Editor: Mona Fertig
Editing: Pearl Luke
Copy Editing: Judith Brand
Typefaces used are Aboriginal Serif and Lato Sans
Printed on paper made of material from well-managed FSC®-certified forests, recycled materials,
and other controlled sources
Printed and bound in Canada

Mother Tongue Publishing gratefully acknowledges the assistance of the Province of British
Columbia through the B.C. Arts Council and we acknowledge the support of the Canada Council
for the Arts, which last year invested $153 million to bring the arts to Canadians throughout the
country. Nous remercions le Conseil des arts du Canada de son soutien. L'an dernier, le Conseil a
investi 153 millions de dollars pour mettre de l'art dans la vie des Canadiennes et des Canadiens de
tout le pays.

LIBRARY AND ARCHIVES CANADA CATALOGUING IN PUBLICATION

Title: Love of the Salish Sea Islands : new essays, memoirs and poems by 40 island writers : a
    treasury of writing celebrating the beauty, community and importance of our archipelagos.
Identifiers: Canadiana 20190090561 | ISBN 9781896949734 (softcover)
Subjects: LCSH: Island life—British Columbia—Pacific Coast—Literary collections. | LCSH: Island
    life—Northwest, Pacific—Literary collections. | LCSH: Islands—Salish Sea (B.C. and Wash.)—
    Literary collections. | LCSH: Islands—British Columbia—Pacific Coast—Literary collections. |
    LCSH: Island life—Northwest, Pacific—Anecdotes.
Classification: LCC PS8255.B7 L68 2019 | DDC C810.8/03271131—dc23

To the past, present and future guardians of the islands and waters of the Salish Sea.

CONTENTS

INTRODUCTION

On Duncan Avenue in downtown Courtenay on Vancouver Island, I recently noticed the words "Be the spirit of a place" in white painted script on the wall of a building.

The early writings of a contributor to this book—Jack Hodgins— helped me learn about the spirit of that place, the Comox Valley.

Back in the late 1970s, I felt proud to identify as a "trench dweller," a notion Hodgins introduced in his collection of stories called *Spit Delaney's Island,* referring to people living in the area between the Coast Mountains and the Vancouver Island mountain ranges. Hodgins, like me, had grown up in the Comox Valley and put our earthy culture forged from the sea, forests and farms on its own brightly lit stage for the first time.

I still feel as awed by the beauty of "the trench" as I did when Hodgins' stories first piqued awareness of my childhood home, although the Comox Valley has changed radically since the time of my and Hodgins' respective youths.

Salt Spring Island has also inevitably changed since I moved here in 1985, with the population almost doubling, but the essential spirit of the place has not changed. I am grateful not only for the years I have spent on Salt Spring, where my ideal life partner was waiting for me and our daughter was born and raised, but for the opportunity to visit a number of other Salish Sea islands. Each one is absolutely distinct from the others, and *Love of the Salish Sea Islands* celebrates that diversity.

Gratitude and a desire to inspire an ethic of preservation are two reasons Mona Fertig of Mother Tongue Publishing instigated this collection of new poems, essays and memoirs touching all shorelines in the Salish Sea region.

In light of the threats the islands face from climate change and development pressures, Fertig wanted to create a legacy of the archipelago —from Quadra in the north to Lummi in the south—as it exists in 2019 and a gift for everyone who loves islands. She wanted the book to be "a small taste of island life, and why we treasure islands, and why we shouldn't take them for granted, with the tiny hope that the natural beauty and non-conformist nature of islands and islanders will never be lost, destroyed or negatively exploited."

Fertig has clearly succeeded in her mission.

Something I appreciate about this anthology is that the writers' love of the islands does not gush, as some visitors or newcomers are wont to do. Reverence is the more dominant strain of affection, I'd say. It has grown slowly from the writers' time spent on beaches, in boats and on trails among the Douglas-fir and arbutus trees, or from the first stirrings of understanding about Indigenous ways of being, practised among the islands for thousands of years.

Then there's the inescapable physical challenges of living on an island. It can be difficult to wrestle with the topography, the ferries, the lack of amenities and tradespeople who respond promptly, and the psychological isolation, for some. But for island dwellers who have found a place that feeds their spirit, their need for community and wonder in the natural world, and lets them wear pajamas to the grocery store without anyone batting an eye, the struggles gradually slough away. The *Love of the Salish Sea Islands* authors acknowledge both the challenges and the rewards of island life.

This compilation also makes me think about the ideas Peter Wohlleben illuminates in his book *The Hidden Life of Trees*, which draws on research from the University of British Columbia's forestry department. We now know that trees communicate with and send nutrients to each other through their roots and fungal systems. Similarly, the pieces in *Love of the Salish*

Sea Islands share the wisdom and nourishment of island experiences, strengthening our connections and the resiliency of the whole region, through underwater literary channels.

These days many people are asking themselves what they can do to slow the destructive path our world seems to be travelling on.

Love of the Salish Sea Islands gives us some direction. Aim to be like Steven Ross Smith paddling in his poem *"Buoyed"*–"one with the Salish Sea." Settle into the islands' "folds of peace," as Fertig suggests. Be the slow and quiet spirit of the islands. Be humbled. Be reverent. Be awed.

— Gail Sjuberg, Salt Spring Island

TAIAIAKE ALFRED

TUMBO ISLAND

TEMOSEN

There is a tiny island shouting distance from Saturna in the Salish Sea that has a hold on me. Hardly more than an anvil-shaped outcrop, it has steep cliffs with forested high ground on the long edges, a rocky beach on one end and a natural harbour with tidal mud flats on the other. The middle part of the island is all marsh. That is all there is to it, save for the play of light and mist that rises so exquisitely when the sun shines down on the wet ground. And wildlife too, plenty of deer and hundreds of geese. Naturally, it is a small speck of perfection.

No human presence remains on the island, or rather, there are only remnants, an old house and collapsing barn abandoned a century ago. When I am there, amidst the collapsed settlement and nature taking back her rock, I feel fully immersed in an unfolding, uncertain and ancient future.

My connection to the island started with an invitation from my friend Xumtholt, a scholar, hunter and fisherman from the Tsawout First Nation. Xumtholt and others from the W̱SÁNEĆ Nation hunt deer on the island, as is their birthright and pleasure. The first time I went with him, I asked about the name of the island, and he told me that it is called Tumbo Island on the map. I let that word roll around in my head while we slowly made our way in his small boat through the fog, past all the islands in the channel between Sidney and the open part of the strait.

When we approached our island and landed on the shore, I jumped out of the boat and walked up the small incline leading from the beach and took in the view. Struck by the perfection of the little treasure, my mind couldn't accept that name: *Tumbo*. It sounded too trivial for such a special place. His boat anchored on the beach, Xumtholt and I talked about this as he took me over to a Parks Canada sign that had been placed a short ways inland. There we read that the walking path that traversed the island had been named the Temosen Trail. No explanation for the name of the trail was given. We didn't need any.

Temosen is the name held by a respected elder in the W̱SÁNEĆ Nation, a master carver, Xumtholt's uncle and my good friend. Names are sacred for

Indigenous People, and it is not my right to share the meaning of the man's name or talk about it. But, it is most definitely ancient, certainly dignified and obviously connected through a thick storyline to the island. Xumtholt and I, in that moment, renamed the tiny island Temosen Island, a befitting name. With Xumtholt's sharing of his nation's heritage, the island has, gratefully for me, become a place where I can feel connected with the ancestral spirits that are grounded in the land and pulsing through the waters of this territory.

There is usually no one else on the island, and we have it to ourselves. The few people we have occasionally run into have seemed nervous about being alone on an island with us and haven't stayed long or just got back in their boat and left for having caught sight of us—brown guys with bows and arrows! We like it like that. I've thought about it a lot on the boat rides to and from Temosen, and I think we go to the island so we can experience being Indigenous in a place where there are no constant and overwhelming human-formed reminders of how very difficult it is to be Indigenous. We're drawn to the idea of it as a space where we can transgress and escape the regulated feeling of the places we have to live our lives every other day, free to live out in a small way our own imagined Indigenous selves.

For Xumtholt, me and my 11-year-old son, being Indigenous means walking the land hunting. One late summer afternoon, we set out on the footpath that leads from the beach. I tell my son that we are Natives doing Native things on Native land, and that I am proud and grateful to be here with him and Xumtholt because this time and place and togetherness is a gift. We walk quietly along the path to a place Xumtholt thinks we will see deer, and he is right. He raises his fist, and we stop and scan the field of tall grass ahead. In the shade of a willow, we can see ears flicking just above the tops of the grass. We look at each other and smile and then crouch down to shield ourselves from their view. The deer sense us. They stand, look our way, and in a heartbeat, two does bound away from us on a trail that runs along the edge of the marsh. Xumtholt takes the low route, and me and my son double-back on the trail. We are not long on the trail before my son spots one of the deer in a small thicket and tells me so. I don't see it myself, but I trust his eyes and tell him to sit on the trail and wait and watch for movement. I turn back toward the bush and approach it carefully, knowing that a wild animal is in there, poised to escape, and just waiting to sense laxness in me. I am ten yards away from the thicket, crouching, and still don't see anything moving. Then the deer jumps out of the bush high right in front of me, and though my heart is in my throat, when it hits the ground, I shoot it dead. We are blessed.

Xumtholt rejoins us on the higher ground, and there are smiles and handshakes and respect to the spirit of the deer. As we gut and skin and butcher the animal and carry the meat back to the beach, my son listens to me and Xumtholt tell stories about hunters who have come here before us and of our own hunts on this island and in other places. And the beauty of it all is that we are all on our own: Natives doing something Native on Native land, asking no one's permission and answering only to the spirits of the land and the ancestral teachings of the long line of hunters who have come before us. My son is now part of that tradition himself, and he's become a resurgent Indigenous presence on the island.

Being on Temosen is powerful salve on the soul scarring caused by the disconnection from nature and each other that marks the everyday existence we all endure. It is medicine, and our visits are a kind of ritual of reclaiming, renaming and represencing to strengthen our spirits so we don't completely lose ourselves under the constant pressure of whiteness bearing down on us. Hunting on Temosen is necessary to my son and me as a form of resistance against the loss we feel and must always carry inside, a result of the cutting of crucial connections that root us in place and tie us to land. Our relationship with the W̱SÁNEĆ through Xumtholt and Temosen, their sharing of teachings and rites, has given us self-awareness as Indigenous People in relation to them and this place and is helping me show my son pathways to meaning and purpose as a respectful human being living on the edge of the Salish Sea.

CHRIS ARNETT

SALT SPRING ISLAND

FUNERAL FOR A DOG

You don't have to look far to see that there is a dearth of Salish voice in this volume, especially considering the fact that the Salish, as we call them, have lived here for at least 10,000 years. This reflects the current demographic and cultural reality of the islands with newcomers far outnumbering the original residents. Even the word *Salish* is a misnomer, it being the correct name of the Indigenous People in present-day Idaho, who just happened to be the speakers of a broad language group dubbed Salish by outsiders now insiders.

Indigenous culture—a way of viewing the world—is not always apparent unless you know where to look and what to look for. Knowing "what was" and "what is," we can fathom "what is possible." This is an old teaching applicable to anything.

People have lived on Salt Spring Island for so long that there is a soil type called Neptune that is the accumulated dark sediment of people and their activities in a single location over thousands of years. Some of these deposits are meters deep and cover acres of land. Hul'q'umi'num' speakers call them *stl'ulnup*, a word that means "a covered (thus ancient) ground." An elder described them as cemeteries (*smukw'elu*, "place to have funerals and containers for bodies") because, over millennia of occupation, the people occasionally buried there became in effect part of the soil. If you know where to look, you can see these deposits, thick and thin, in the physical shape of the land

If this physical continuity exists with the ancient past, can the same be said of its spiritual component believed to be a part of this world? Chief Seattle, in his famous 1854 speech in the city that bears his name, told the settlers of his land that even if the Indigenous People disappeared entirely, the white man would never be alone, given that the land (water, rocks, trees, animals etc.) was sentient and populated by the numerous dead who live in what can best be described as a parallel world. He admonished settlers to be just with his people because the dead were not powerless and could at times, if they chose, intervene in the affairs of the living.

19

The phone rang in the 1990s, and it was Tim, my 50-something friend and neighbour down the road. "Hey, Chris. I just wanted to let you know that Toby got hit by a car last night." Toby was Tim's elderly black spaniel whatever island mix with a mangy coat and a red collar. "Oh no," I said trying to sound empathetic. "Yeah, I took her to the vet, but there was nothing he could do... anyhow I'm having a little wee get-together at my place for a wee memorial."

"Ok, we'll be there," I said, meaning that *I* would be there, and as usual, Barbara would stay home with our two little boys. She was not into sitting outside around a smoky fire on a rainy winter night drinking and smoking at a funeral for a dog.

We lived a couple of driveways down on Fulford-Ganges Road, a two-lane asphalt super-highway between the Fulford Harbour ferry terminal and Ganges, the commercial centre of the island. Fulford-Ganges Road had long stretches conducive to high speed for those racing to catch a ferry or racing to get home from it. You could tell the time of day by the boatload of traffic that raced by every hour and a half. Just after we moved here in 1988, the road claimed the life of our beloved Wee-Wee, a sleek black cat that had no problem following me around for blocks off 4th Ave in Kitsilano but was totally unprepared for a rural life where a quiet country road would suddenly erupt with tons of speeding metal.

After supper I went to the root cellar and retrieved a bottle of homemade blackberry wine. I headed up our steep driveway and along the widened shoulder that served as a path along Fulford-Ganges.

Tim lived a few addresses down at one end of a steep curve that occasionally propelled various speeding cars and trucks into his front yard. He slowly built up a barrier with berms and trees that gave some semblance of protection, but not for Toby, the latest victim on the pet-killer highway.

Tim's place, a small cabin with a porch on a small lot was the social centre of a neighourhood of hippies and self-employed working folk who lived around the misty meadows of Ford Lake. The old farm before the area was subdivided was called Mereside by an early settler, in reference to the spooky mist (the mere) that hung heavy on the lake, as it did tonight.

It was dark and raining softly—not too cold. A large fire of wood scraps salvaged from Tim's various carpentry projects blazed in the yard near the house, making a comfortable dome of heat for the folks gathered around it.

I knew most of the people there, fellow settlers recolonizing the inland reaches of the island, including my friends, the nice hippy couple (he from West Van, she from Ontario) who lived next door to Tim on a small acreage. Resourceful types, they had a large garden and sold weed. Also present was Bette from Quebec who had recently arrived on Salt Spring as a single mother with two toddlers—now a self-employed gardener building her own house on a challenging lot in a steep ravine. And George and his partner, Pat, sat together, both older artists but pioneers in the new world of personal computers. There were a few others, regulars to the scene, come and gone. Tim greeted me warmly as always. In spite of the occasion, he was his jovial self as he grinned and opened another bottle of McEwan's.

By the fire, I saw someone I didn't recognize, a tall lanky guy in dark clothing who wore his black hair long around his face. Tim introduced us. Robert had recently met Katherine, another neighbor of Tim. Both now lived in a "land yacht," a mobile home built by her ex and parked next door for nominal rent. Katherine began to tell me that Robert was an apprentice medicine man.

We had only been on the island a few years adjusting to the *eclectic*, which denotes a school of philosophers who picked and chose their doctrines. I'd met many people of this sort on the island from all backgrounds and had developed an automatic non-empathy whenever I encountered this philosophy and its followers. I felt the same about this dog memorial.

Robert and I engaged in a long discussion. Back then we talked about "native stuff" as if we knew. I asked him about his people, and he said that he was not sure who they were. A victim of the 60s scoop, he thought he might be from the Prairies. It wasn't apparent to either of us that Indigenous culture cannot be reduced to this or that. It is a process. Might take a thousand years.

Tim spoke up from where he was standing across the fire and asked Robert if he would like to perform the ceremony. I hadn't anticipated a ceremony. Because Robert was studying to be "a medicine man," he had been chosen to perform the rites.

This is very *saltspring*, I thought, and not in a good way.

When he turned to me and asked, "What should I do?" I told him we should throw some of Toby's dog food into the fire.

Robert relayed this to Tim who bounded up the stairs into the house and came out with a half-empty bowl of dry dog food, which he gave to Robert. He took the bowl and poured some of it into Tim's hand and gestured that he must throw it into the fire. We stood silent around the fire, faces bathed in its light against the dark night beyond. I did not feel solemn but rather amused, almost to the point of laughter, not helped by the sweet wine and that potent pot from the place next door.

As Tim knelt on his knees and looked into the flames, his wire-rimmed glasses blazed in the light. All was quiet except the crackling fire. Tim tossed the dog food into the flames and immediately dropped his head to the ground, sobbing heavily and loudly. The smirk disappeared from my face. You have to know what was and what is, to know what is possible.

BRENDA BROOKS

SALT SPRING ISLAND

VIEW OF YOU

(FROM FERNWOOD DOCK)

I wish I could be yours always,
like some poor slob's love letter torn to shreds
and tossed overboard, or a doomed gull
swept away on a savage updraft. Or how about that
demolished log—a proud coastal fir wrenched
off its feet by one of your many tirades.

Forgive my excess, but it's you
who seduced and brought the drama out in me.

And so, I wish you had followed through,
claimed me outright, made me your own,
left me trashed like the wrecked bow of a boat
washed up in one of your secret coves,
gone to pieces among the bleached shells
of ravaged oysters, my bones an abandoned
bonfire extinguished by your slow, silken tide—

you get my drift.

I guess what I'm trying to say is:
even now I long to be taken by you,
bent and broken into something deeper,
something oceans away from myself,
true to you always.

But I'm only a sorry human,
(elusive as you) come down to your island shore
with a bottle of red to toast you
and tell you goodbye

and that I'll miss you and remember, now and then,
(once safely inland) your salty, seductive lips,
and how easy it would have been
on certain blue-stained days,
to wade in waist-deep—and further still
and take you in my arms

and be forever yours.

MARIA COFFEY

PROTECTION ISLAND, LASQUETI ISLAND

SWIMMING THE SALISH SEA

I first arrived on a Salish Sea island in a disgruntled mood, wishing I were somewhere else. Some months before, I had applied for a teacher exchange position in Canada, and I requested a school in or close to Vancouver. My focus was mountains; I dreamed of skiing every spare minute in the winter, of hiking in the summer. A woman from the exchange agency in London called to say that a perfect match had just come up; the only glitch was that my placement school was "a bit of a way" from Vancouver, in a town whose name she struggled to pronounce.

"Na-neee-moo," she said. "But apparently it's only about twenty-five miles from Vancouver as the crow flies."

There was nothing closer, I was anxious for a change, and the potential exchange teacher needed an answer. I accepted on the spot. By the time I realized that a sizeable stretch of water lay between Vancouver and Nanaimo, it was too late to change my mind.

I flew into Vancouver on a perfect August day. As the plane started its final approach, I pressed my face to the window, gazing landwards to the jagged peaks of the mainland, and barely noticing the glittering sea dotted with islands below. A few days later, as a ferry took me across that sea to Vancouver Island, I stood on the stern deck sadly watching the range of mountains grow smaller across the horizon.

Nanaimo appalled me. I hated the small-town mentality, the smell of the pulp and paper mill, the lonely suburb where I lived. So busy hating everything, I overlooked the pretty harbour and beaches. I only went near the waterfront at weekends to catch the Vancouver ferry and, when ski season started, to head onward to Whistler.

I had every intention of escaping Nanaimo the moment my one-year teaching exchange ended. Then, in February, I met Dag. He had arrived in Nanaimo from Germany a few months earlier than me, to do his PhD research at the

Pacific Biological Station, which overlooked the Salish Sea. When we first went out for a beer, he raved about how fabulous his summer had been, and all the swimming he had done. He told me he had just rented a cabin on a small island in Nanaimo Harbour, and invited me over there.

A few days later, Dag rowed me a mile across the harbour to Protection Island. On the way, he shared his plans for getting into kayaking and sailing. Already smitten with this man, I didn't want to scare him off by admitting my terror of deep water. Over a decade earlier, during a holiday in Morocco with three friends, I had nearly drowned in the Atlantic. On a beach near the village where we were staying, we had joined a group of young travellers bodysurfing in the breaking waves. I was a weak swimmer, but it all seemed easy and safe. Then a man swam out beyond the surf break, and appeared to be in trouble. People formed a chain to try to reach him. Instinctively I reached out a hand, and suddenly I was part of the line, moving into chest-high water. A huge wave rolled in, crashed over us and broke the line apart. I remember being tumbled around, as if in a washing machine, then surfacing and realizing that I too was beyond the break. My efforts to swim in were futile; no matter how hard I tried, the shore receded. I saw my friends gesticulating, their mouths opening with shouts I couldn't hear above the roar of the surf. Waves slammed against my face; I inhaled, gagged, flailed, tried to take a breath and inhaled more. I didn't know then that I had been caught in a rip current. That eventually it would curl around, and bring me back to the shallows. All I knew, in the loneliest moment of my life, was that I was helpless against the force of the ocean. That I was dying.

On the beach, confusion reigned. Someone ran to the village for help, others started dragging a small fishing boat toward the water. The man we had attempted to rescue swam in safely. And I had disappeared from sight. Then I was spotted, washing about in the surf at the far end of the bay; I was hauled ashore, blue tinged and not breathing. A group gathered around me and had frantic discussions about resuscitation methods; they tried everything and eventually something worked.

In medieval times, the European name for the Atlantic was *Mare Tenebrosum,* and in Arabic it was known as *Bahr al-Zulamat.* Both translate to "Sea of

Darkness," feared for its raging storms, its unpredictable winds and its unforgiving waves in which countless souls had perished. Since my mishap, I shared that ancient fear; the sea—any sea—had become a dark place that I avoided. As Dag rowed toward Protection Island, chatting happily about the future, I didn't tell him all this; instead I smiled and held onto the boat's gunnels in a white-knuckled grip.

Winter turned to spring. I got used to crossing the harbour, and spent my weekends with Dag on Protection. In the mid-1980s, this sliver of land had a small population living in cabins tucked among sizeable stands of second-growth forest. We followed tiny winding paths through the trees to the waterfront, which was hardly developed. For hours we explored the rocky shorelines, peering into tidal pools, watching sea birds, collecting stones and interesting driftwood. On clear nights, we lay out in sleeping bags to stargaze and listen to the lapping waves. I came to appreciate the pungent smells of low tide, the sound of suckling barnacles, the freshness of salt air. My need for the mountains faded; I was happy on the island with my new love.

Early summer came and Dag started swimming. By then I had told him my drowning story. I wanted to get past my fears, and he promised to help me. In the calm waters of the channel between Protection and Newcastle Islands, I waded in and took a few strokes. When I tried to touch down and felt only water under my feet, a visceral fear of the deep gripped me, and I thrashed back to safety. Gradually, by telling myself that land was in easy reach, I could swim in circles out of my depth. I relaxed enough to watch great blue herons skim by, their long legs trailing behind them then flexing as they landed on nearby rocks. I laughed when seals popped up their heads to curiously regard me, before sliding beneath the water's surface again, nose last. But I couldn't face submerging my own head. I swam with it poking up on an uncomfortably elongated neck.

Dag had a favourite spot on the north side of Protection Island, where he could jump off the rocks into deep water. One sunny July day, I decided to be brave and join him. Jumping wasn't an option for me, so he found a place where I could step from rock to rock under the water then launch into a swimming position. I stepped, squatted and pushed off into a breaststroke. A ferry had steamed by, and when its wake reached us, waves started rebounding from the shoreline. As they tossed me about, I kept my eyes on the mainland mountains, determined to stay calm. Dag swam backwards, watching and encouraging me. Later he said he would never forget how my face changed when a wave slapped against it, how terror flooded my features. I started choking and windmilling my limbs, unravelled by flashes of memory, by the trauma that resided deep in my body rising up to engulf me. Had I been alone, I might have drowned right there, but Dag guided me back to shore and calmed me down.

We returned to the gentle waters of the channel. I counted my strokes—ten away from shore, then twenty, then thirty, then fifty and back. A woman I befriended on the island became my other coach. Barbara Jane patiently swam alongside me every day, encouraging me to put my head under the water, to swim a bit farther, and farther still. Late that summer, when finally I swam the 300 meters across to Newcastle Island, and back again, she applauded me as if I had broken an Olympic record.

By the following spring, Dag and I were living together on Protection Island, in a tiny waterfront cabin perched on a low bluff. We had no running water, so every morning we would roll out of bed, clamber down the rough-hewn rock steps and jump—yes, jump—into the Salish Sea. That would be the first of several swims during the day, often with an extra one at night. Ah, those night swims. I first witnessed bioluminescence from Dag's boat, when its movement through the water caused tiny creatures to emit their light. That had been astonishing enough, but swimming in it was like being dropped into fairyland. I could see the outline of Dag's shape, as if enveloped by stars, with me a watery Tinker Bell, in a cloud of pixie dust. On clear new moon nights, when the Milky Way stretched above us, it was as if sea and sky had merged and I floated in both. To be swimming without fear in deep, dark water was a miracle in itself, but nothing had prepared me for such astounding, transcendent beauty.

Dag and I married and settled on Protection Island. We built a little beachfront house with a separate sauna. Over the next two decades, on many winter nights we ran from the sauna into the cold sea, then sat steaming on the shore. Protection got developed around us, and eventually we moved to Lasqueti, a more remote Salish Sea island. There Dag built a hot tub in the rocks close to the water's edge, and we had eleven more years of magical night swims through bioluminescence.

But the best swim always was—and still is—the first of the day. Right after waking up, before coffee, our eyes not yet fully open, our feet remembering their way across the rocky beach. At the shoreline, Dag plunging straight in and away, his arms arcing through a strong crawl. For me, a slower entry, feeling the silky water rise against my skin, until the moment of surrender, trusting my body to float, my limbs to propel. Immersing my head, then shaking drops from my eyes, seeing the luminous sky, the light playing across the ripples of the sea. All anxieties dissolving in a flood of elation and optimism. Each of these morning swims is like a blessing. A daily renewal. An addictive drug of the healthiest kind. Life has taken us back to Vancouver Island; on calm mornings we walk from our home in downtown Victoria to a special pocket beach, and plunge into some of the coldest waters of the Salish Sea.

And now life has brought me back to Morocco, to the beach where I almost drowned. From where I am writing this, I can look across to the breaking Atlantic waves, to surf foaming across the sand, to the very spot where I lay sprawled as my chest was thumped and, with ragged gasps, I began to breathe again.

Yesterday, with Dag, I swam in my sea of darkness. We checked that the rip wasn't running. We went beyond the surf break, into deep waters where the swell lazily lifted us as it rolled in. Then we rode the waves back to shore. Once I mistimed: glancing over my shoulder, I saw a wave rearing up right behind me, its clear blue belly topped by a high frothing crest. It smashed down, tossing me about like a rag doll, but I relaxed in its turbulence, knowing it would soon release me. Back on the beach, I stood quietly for a while, grateful for how easily air moved through my lungs, for the second chance I was given, for all that has happened since then.

I think of my life like an ocean current. It brought me, at first unwillingly, to the Salish Sea. Often it has taken me away again, around the world, for long stretches of time. But always it tugs me back to that glittering sea dotted with islands: the place where love and courage grew, where big adventures began, where swimming became a spiritual necessity. Nowhere else do I feel as safe, joyful and centred as in the waters and on the shorelines of the Salish Sea. It is and always will be my Sea of Light.

Aftas Beach, Morocco, January 4, 2019

DANIEL COWPER

BOWEN ISLAND

PAINTING WITH WATER

Wanting to blast our coastline
to navvyjack, miners navelled rock
with holes to slip the charges in—
now, high tides rinse the unused sheaths,

leave them full when sinking back.
Arbutus saplings draggle off
the tops of creosoted pilings now,
where barges were meant

but never moored. Kids drying
on the rockface wet their pointers
in the drillholes' warmth, paint
figures in dark lines of moisture

the sun sucks up as fast as their fingers
can pattern them. Fingers dip
into little wells to retint

the withering image, while the moon
draws the fringed tide uphill
to drown the naked stone.

THE NEW LIFE

With you in the wild goose nest I knew it would be so,
that night we swam through a forest lake. Tired halfway, you clung

on my slippery back until we reached a floating platform of weeds
where geese had hatched their clutch, where goslings

had swum and fledged. We kissed and caressed on that buoyant mat—
our skins burnt off their sheaths of slickness. You shivered

but that shiver and our hands and lips were all that moved.
Dante rightly called this New. In the goose nest I knew I'd stepped

from one world to the next—new rules applying, old labels
of risk and safety flipped. Why was this so effortless to sense?

Now you've trapped within taut abdomen a living apple seed,
dots where eyes should be, webs between its digits. Blood glues

this swelling pupa to your womb, fulfilling our union. With you
in the wild goose nest, I knew it would be so.

WILLIAM DEVERELL

PENDER ISLAND

MY ISLAND, MY MUSE

As I compose these notes, the bells have rung in the new year of 2019, which may or may not be worth celebrating, given the perilous state of our planet. I find more comfort in raising a glass to the past, because this year marks my fortieth anniversary living on a little sylvan island—six miles long and three wide—called North Pender.

The reward for my staying power is that I have finally attained the lofty rank of old-timer. There is a higher class, to which it is hopeless to aspire, of seniors born or raised here. And there are several levels of lesser nobility: full-time residents, weekend cottagers, visitors, vacation renters and, of lowest rank, the yahoos who think it's okay to bomb around on country roads tossing beer cans and plastic wrappers.

Our house, a star-shaped cedar octagon that some locals call the White Man's Tepee, is also celebrating its fortieth anniversary—after a PTSD-inducing difficult birth, sired by hippie handcrafters, artists, designers, and itinerant musicians.

I wrote my first novel in this house: *Needles*, which was also born in 1979. So that was a hell of a year, a life-changer. Until then the notion seemed absurd that I could escape the burdens of a law practice and earn a living—in Canada!—writing novels.

Until the 1970s, I had never set foot on a Gulf Island, though was intrigued by the mystery of those placid green humps gliding past the ferry. What manner of weird loner would live there? What was there to *do*? How does one survive without theatres, concert halls, galleries, cocktail bars?

Growing up on the Prairies, I'd hungered for the vibrant life of the city, the noisier and brighter the better, and Vancouver fit me like a well-tailored suit. I was fighting famous trials, working hard, living hard, getting ink—it helped that I was a former *Sun* reporter—while somehow finding the time to be a husband and father.

But after two decades as a partner in a hyperactive, ego-driven law firm, a kind of malaise seeped in, a discomfort that I refused to blame on overwork and the grinding, competitive tension that is peculiar to the legal profession and that regularly causes breakdowns.

Within me, something did snap, but oddly, and softly, and it occurred on my first visit to a Gulf Island, to see a couple who had abandoned the comfort and glamour of Vancouver for Salt Spring—I could only assume they'd gone bonkers, and was all but certain when I saw goats being shooed from the deck of their ramshackle country home and chickens from the kitchen.

As I wandered about their small acreage, a strange peace settled over me, a slowing. Attuned to the jangling of the city, I felt disoriented by the trilling entreaties of woodland sparrows; the high-rises from which they sang were not dead structures but alive, breathing, propagating: statuesque cedars and firs and flouncy, gay arbutuses.

I am not what one would call a spiritual person, and worship no god or prophet, but rather suffer the uncompromising insolence of the hard-core rationalist. So I lack the tools and gifts of those, like my new-age friends, that might help explain this transformative event on Salt Spring Island.

Maybe Dr. Freud could help. Maybe some repressed yearning flowered. I knew deeply, in any event, that I was not enduring some starry-eyed back-to-the-land whimsy. I wanted this. I wanted all of this. This peace. That birdsong. That crook-backed bigleaf maple leaning over the pond. That rickety bench and rickety fence. The sense of being on an island, a moated bolthole, bridgeless, untethered to the fat, swelling city.

That summer, I spent my every free day exploring the Southern Gulf Islands, travelling their back roads, being pitched to by eager, chatty realtors and during evenings pouring through the classifieds.

My wife and I finally chose ten forested acres on North Pender with an open field suitable for gardening. The price was right. The American seller was convinced that Dave Barrett's newly elected socialist government planned to confiscate foreign-owned properties—through the device of the grasping monster known as the Agricultural Land Reserve Commission. There seemed no point taking issue with the views of this stubborn Republican, or to confess that Barrett was a pal and one of my heroes.

For one thing, his government saved the Gulf Islands from ruin by creating the Islands Trust, with its mandate to preserve and protect the islands' unique ecology. For another, I am proud that our land is within the ALR, indivisible, undisturbed but for dwelling and outbuildings. The cabin where I write this lies underneath a canopy of carbon-capturing coniferous giants.

The property was originally intended as a retreat from the city (I too was once a weekender), but as the island continued its charm offensive the weekends expanded, ultimately encompassing Thursday nights through Monday mornings. (Many judges are easily persuaded to adjourn trials set for Fridays.)

We began, as many newcomers do, making friends, a task at which Penderites are peculiarly adept—and I include the amiable outliers of South Pender, our smaller sibling over the bridge—and many of these friends were in the building trades, jaunty and assertive: "We can have this sucker up, roofed, plumbed, septic done, in six months easy."

Four years later, its shell was sitting abandoned after two sets of contractors were sent packing, as costs mounted faster than the posts and beams. The third, a jovial, bearded, beer-loving Limey named Patrick Brownrigg arrived like a rescuing angel to finish it in time for my planned year's sabbatical.

That's where I pounded out *Needles* on a typewriter, under a nest of massive inclining sawn cedars that seemed to fortify me with pyramid power. My other nineteen books and innumerable scripts and screenplays were written there or in this studio.

So you, my green-gowned lady, my lovely, lusty, busty Aphrodite with your coves and bluffs and winding trails—you, my island, have been my muse.

Yet it was almost twenty years after you set my life on this creative course and away from the cold, pitiless dialectic of the law that I honoured you. In 1997, finally, I recreated you as a continuing character, under the nom de plume of Garibaldi Island, in *Trial of Passion*. A novel in which a stressed and trial-weary criminal lawyer escapes Vancouver (or tries to) for a new life on the soothing shores of the Salish Sea.

Garibaldi Island stars in six successive novels, including the one in progress. The agony prompted by the halting efforts to build the White Man's Tepee has found its reward in the sketching of several recurring characters (e.g., Stoney and Dog) drawn from my laid-back, pot-puffing work crew, all forgiven friends.

Many other characters, especially from my early days on Pender, have reappeared, often poorly disguised. A postmaster, for instance, who read aloud the back of postcards before yielding them to their rightful recipients. A Green Party leader who many confuse with Elizabeth May. A dimwit former trustee, a pawn of developers.

It's a struggle to preserve and protect the islands of the Salish Sea from those whose vision of them is clouded by dollar signs, a struggle that engages conservationists, especially over issues involving the threatened loss of carrying capacity of land and water resources.

Those, like me, who have attained old-timer status and have paid our dues as stewards, do not feel disparaged when accused of trying to pull up the drawbridge. It is often overlooked that the legislated object of the Trust is to preserve these islands for the enjoyment of *all* residents of British Columbia. Tourism matters on the Gulf Islands. Tourists don't come here to marvel at condos and subdivisions.

Thankfully, we endure drawbacks that deter unsustainable growth—the cost of ferries, the frequent power blackouts (just before Christmas, a ferocious windstorm downed power lines for up to ten days here on Pender), the restricted choice of entertainment venues. (Mind you, this island is blessed with an incalculable number of community groups and events and a wealth of talent.)

Many Canadians have never come nearer to farm, field or forest than while rocketing along the 401. An example: several years ago, a Toronto literary agent who was vying for my business stepped off the ferry dressed for a royal wedding and, gaping, expostulated: "This has got to be the end of the world!" We put him up in our guest cottage in the woods, jokingly telling him that he need not fear bears, wolves or cougars or even old Elmore, who is slightly touched but merely likes to peer through windows at night.

The poor fellow took us seriously and slept not a wink, with all the lights blazing. Elmore never showed up. The agent never came back.

Oh, well.

ANN ERIKSSON

GALIANO ISLAND, RETREAT ISLAND, THETIS ISLAND

INSPIRATION ISLAND

Seven acres. Give or take a few rocks. A big old rock itself. A crewcut of trees. A hundred shades of green. You walk the path from the house you helped to build, along the top of the cliff with its scrub of Garry oaks, a wave of blue-eyed Mary and yellow monkey flower cascading down. You duck under the arching arbutus, check in on the Indian paintbrush decorating your old summer campsite, lean against the rough heavy bark of the Douglas-fir so you can peer down from a height into the sea. A moon jelly sails by. The purple and orange arms of sea stars peek out from crevices. The previous day a neighbour phoned to alert you to the killer whales heading your way, and you had stopped everything to watch them pass, their black dorsal fins cutting through the sea, rising and falling as they traveled. You wondered if they'd known you were there.

You take a detour into the backside forest to say good morning to the ephemeral calypso orchids with their graceful bowed heads. Now tightrope walk along the ridge of the reef down to the shell beach. The emerald fronds of an eelgrass meadow call to you from the bay. You strip off your clothes and dive in. So cold you gasp and race back to shore. Every cell of your body wakes up. A great blue heron croaks and lifts from the beach across the way. You spread your body on the smooth sandstone shelf. The surface rough and warm on your skin. Beside you, a tide pool of aggregate anemones opens like flowers.

Above you the sky shines clear and blue. A bald eagle soars overhead, hunting for fish or ducklings. You marvel at how you got here, prairie girl. Not born for a coastal life. 1974. On your way to New Zealand to work on a farm after high-school graduation in Edmonton, you took a train trip through the Rocky Mountains to the coast, then the ferry to Victoria to visit your travelling companion's grandmother. You stood together on the deck of the ship the whole way, the wind blowing your hair. The salt air in your nostrils. Life full of possibility and wonder. The world beckoned. The ship slowed to transit a narrow pass between two islands. Homes came into view, wood and glass, tucked into coves and hovering atop cliffs, cradled by trees, and all around water, water and more salt water. A cloud of white birds with black-tipped wings rose from the current ahead of the ship and swirled into the air. Seals grunted their way down a knob of rock and rolled off into the sun-slashed sea, their sleek round heads bobbing up. You took it all in, thinking to yourself, I'd love to live here.

Four years later you are. Like magic. That very island, the one they call Galiano. The place felt like going back in time. The country store with its oiled wood floor and a pot-bellied stove in the back where the locals drank coffee and gossiped. The mobile vegetable market that set up in the old community hall every Saturday. The dances. The water-witcher who worked for a bottle of whisky and said to you, "Here, let me charge you up," then handed you his forked willow stick, took your hand and roared with laughter when the stick curved up toward the sky instead of down. "Witching rain now are you, girl?" A benevolent German ghost you sometimes heard sighing and rolling over in the guest room, his painting on the wall near the kitchen. The most magical thing of all, that big old rock of green called Retreat Island. Love took you there. Built you a home where you'd be content to die of old age, rocking in a chair on the deck watching the sun sinking scarlet behind blue-grey mountains in the distance. Love gave you a desk with a view up into an eagle's nest, a garden that grew mostly voles, a child. And another, an angel who touched down to earth, then blew as ashes into the sea barely before she'd arrived.

Love took you there. Love lost took you away. You vanish from the reef without a chance to say goodbye, to the calypso, the moon jelly, the sea stars, the Indian paintbrush, the eagles, the Douglas-fir and arbutus, the anemones, the whales. Your heart breaks in two. You wonder how you can breathe anymore. You start a new life on an island so huge it doesn't feel like an island, in a city that doesn't invite you to grow old there. But you have another child, make friends, discover trails to walk with them, learn how to make a living in nature, paddle and sail through the islands where you used to live. The longing never leaves.

Then the crack in your heart let the words come in. They emerge in the night, waking you with their insistence. They linger in the morning, join into sentences, paragraphs, scenes from a past you never intended to revisit. An island with a brush cut of trees. A black sailing boat with the same name as a lost child. Malaika. Angel. You fell on your knees then, you are driven to your knees now. Go away, you say, it's not the right time. You have work, children, a dog to walk. An old house with creaky steps to fix and a lawn to cut. But the words keep coming. A friend saves you with an invitation to join her and others to craft words into works of art. You make the time. It's a matter of salvation. The words pour out of you, a flood of them and fill the pages until there's a novel about an island, an angel floating in the sea, her hair trailing behind her like seaweed. You open a bottle of champagne with your writing friends when the books arrive—a box of them. Holding the first is like cradling a newborn in your arms.

My paddle dips into the waves as I propel my kayak along the coastline. It's been almost thirty years since I left Retreat Island. I can only think about that earlier time in fragments, in the second person, as if "you" is not me. As if the magic that took me there and inspired me to write happened to someone else. But I've continued to create books. I live on another island now: Thetis Island, the smallest of the Gulf Islands served by BC Ferries. Love brought me here too. This time, I'm staying no matter what, going out feet first as they say.

The Gulf Islands could use a big dose of magic right now. On the surface, the sea and the islands of the Salish Sea appear as tranquil and timeless as they did when I lived on Retreat. But all is not well, above or below. I hunt the shallows for the purple sea stars that once coloured these rocky shores in five-armed piles, but they have all but disappeared over the past few years, dissolving to mush over a day or two. A runaway virus, it's thought, perhaps triggered by warmer waters... or something else. I see one, another, three more. The sea stars may be on the rebound, but the underwater landscape remains a wasteland compared to what used to be here. My fingers drift through the water along the hull. The sea is becoming so acidic that shellfish are having difficulty reproducing, their shells dissolving. I scan the channel for dorsal fins. The fish-eating southern resident killer whales are headed for extinction, their chinook salmon prey overfished or unable to spawn. Their bodies are poisoned by toxic chemicals, their underwater environment polluted with boat traffic noise. The kayak glides over a bed of eelgrass, a nursery for fish and invertebrates. The green fronds show signs of wasting disease, brought on by warmer waters. The birds, where are they? Along the coast, the iconic arbutus trees with their twisted limbs and peeling red bark are turning silver grey with death, and the

45

branches of cedars hang brown and lifeless. We don't eat the shellfish anymore.

Gulf Islanders live in the most imperilled ecological zone in the province, the Coastal Douglas-fir zone, half of it permanently lost to roads, towns and farms, most of the rest fragmented by logging. More species at risk than any other zone live here, the ocean pummelled by coastal development, overfishing and industrial pollution. Loved to death by its admirers. What's to be done? Some of us in the islands raise money to buy land for conservation, to protect it in perpetuity. We build nest boxes for owls and houses for bats, plant eelgrass beds, restore shorelines, educate one another about where we live, the plants and animals we share our home with. Some of us write letters to government against pipelines and tankers, monster freighters; sign petitions to Save the Whales. Other islanders march for the same things; some get arrested doing it. Climate change moves relentlessly on. It's getting hotter, stormier; sea levels are rising, species disappearing.

When I crave inspiration, like today, I launch my kayak and paddle the coastline of Thetis Island. I look for reasons to hope, for anemones opening like flowers, for the rounded head of a seal, for baby sea stars, for healthy young arbutus. Some sections of land in the Gulf Islands are protected in parks or community nature reserves. A proposal to protect the marine ecosystems of the Salish Sea as the Southern Strait of Georgia National Marine Conservation Area Reserve has been on the books for decades. If truly endowed with solid protections such as no-take and anchorage-free zones, it has the potential to slow down or reverse the damage that has already occurred. It's time to make it happen.

To the southeast, I can see the high ridge of Galiano sloping down toward Retreat Cove. Half of Retreat Island is protected by a conservation covenant. No building, no tree removal, the blue-eyed Mary and calypso orchids left to blow in the wind. The island's been sold. Will the new guardians be as good as the last? I hope the island means as much to them as to me. A little bit of magic in the Salish Sea. Seven acres. Give or take a few rocks.

MONA FERTIG

SAVARY ISLAND

Shawl over the shoulders, fierce faced blonde youth daring life, dancing
        we have all come looking for something
Finding grief has its own fault lines, lat and longitude, spume and bite
           saltedged, stories inherited like the palm of your hand
Willow weeping tragicomic over the back of the chalk painted ghost horse
           statue still but ethereal in fog, barebacked
Not ridden for years except by untutored children sworn not to tell,
        wet silkened watermark, calm, innocence, as if it would save you
She tips her head for you in the misted open field no fences
        she does not leap, ceruse eye
Eagle freelifting ground, wings sounds feather your long hair,
           protect you from harm...*so it is, all beginnings...*

GARY GEDDES

TEXADA ISLAND

CLOSE ENCOUNTERS OF THE WATERY KIND

My destiny as an islander began in 1962, when I was offered a teaching job on Texada Island. Most of my predecessors never completed their term, fleeing back to the city, spooked by the isolation, the locals or both. So, just staying the course, I thought, would constitute a major achievement; offering something faintly resembling an education would put me over the top.

I got the job based on my not-very-stellar degree in English and Philosophy from UBC, so I had no idea what these credentials might have prepared me for, other than a serious case of self-doubt. However, as I had grown up poor and dysfunctional on Commercial Drive in Vancouver, sharing a fold-down couch with my older brother in a dingy flat above a woodworking shop, school had always seemed to me a refuge of sorts, a place to relax with peers and an undemanding set of routines. So, it was no surprise, years later, to imagine myself on the other side of the desk, holding forth, though not without a modicum of terror lurking in the margins of consciousness at my inexperience and ignorance.

Taking the first two ferries up the coast, from Horseshoe Bay to Langdale and Earl's Cove to Saltery Bay was a breeze. However, the last leg, Westview to Texada Island, proved prophetic of what lay ahead for me. Mine was the seventh and final car loaded on the MV *Atrevida*, a narrow, top-heavy, down-at-the-ribs wooden vessel that had seen better days. It looked unstable enough to frighten even Charon, the infamous ferryman of Hades, who ferried the dead across the River Styx, his price of passage a coin to be extracted from the mouth of the deceased. My Volkswagen Beetle hesitated at the top of the ramp, uncertain about its decision; but before it could change its mind, two hefty crew members lifted the back end in the air and swung it into place alongside the other four-wheeled coffins and their miscellany of lost souls.

Blubber Bay, our destination, lay dead ahead, a school and cluster of shacks squatting at the northern tip of Texada Island, where a huge bite had been taken out of the limestone mountainside and shipped south to Vancouver to satisfy an endless appetite for concrete. As Vancouver grew skyward, with its seven- to ten-storey high-rises, Texada Island grew smaller, lighter and more buoyant, probably a blessing, as Aboriginal legend has it that the island rose suddenly from the sea and would someday disappear just as precipitously beneath the waves of Malaspina Strait.

The principal actors in this unfolding drama at Vananda's K-12 school, which I feared might turn into a complete farce, included Patrick McFadden, Roger Gibbard and Don Spragge, known affectionately as "The Rug" because of his mat of tight, curly dark hair. Patrick was an Irishman who claimed to have been in such a hurry to get away from England that he missed Canada by five miles, and who went on to be one of the editors of the film magazine *Take Five* and a journalism prof at Carleton University. Roger, a charming former New Zealand airman and activist, took pleasure amusing party guests by standing upside down on a chair, his weight supported only by one hand. These three stalwarts and their politically engaged wives—Josephine, Margaret and Evelyn respectively (lefties, socialists, communists, take your pick)—were to be my mentors for the next ten months. As a backsliding Baptist, I was definitely due for some ribbing and remoulding. White-haired Jim Minnis, ex-military, new school principal and otherwise known as the "Silver Fox," would serve as antagonist, unapproving of the other lot and certainly unimpressed with the bad influence they had on me. All of this cast my Texada experience, at one level, as an amusing and somewhat theatrical version of *Pilgrim's Progress*, contrary forces competing for the soul of Everyman—or, in my case, Noman.

Texada proved transformative in more ways than I'd expected. Aside from hastening my slide down the slippery slope of disbelief, it enlightened me about the true nature of learning: not the funnel method, where you pour information into the presumably empty head of a recipient, but a genuine shared experience where the mutual search for knowledge comes from admitting one's ignorance and seeking ways to address this sorry state. And, as I was soon to learn, the quickest way to acquire knowledge about a subject is to give yourself the difficult task of trying to teach it.

The students, as it turned out, put up with my ignorance and incompetence as long as they knew I cared and struggled to help them understand the material. Jimmy Bunn was an important exception. A hefty farm lad, who knew about hard work and had experienced life-and-death situations with animals, was more than sceptical about the new teacher. Maybe a little jealous, too, of someone not much older than himself, installed in front of the class with whatever undeserved power the position offered. To demonstrate his disdain for this bungling gringo, Jimmy launched spitballs and paper airplanes out across the classroom, one of the latter landing on my desk. Then there were the grunts and the farting sounds made by expelling air from a cupped hand under his armpit. After six weeks of enduring these interruptions and insults, I emitted a bellow that could be heard from one end of the school to the other.

"DOWN TO THE OFFICE!"

I might have reconsidered this command if I'd taken time to weigh the possible consequences: what if he refuses to go, what will happen when we get there, and how will this situation end? However, I had no time for such deliberations. I was in anger mode, having retreated back to my reptilian brain. As he hauled himself slowly from his desk, I imagined Jimmy Bunn running full speed, an unstoppable force, carrying me right through the wall, like those cartoons of the Road Runner, both of us ending up in a heap on the floor of the Home Ec. room next-door, from which had been wafting the smell of baked apple pies all morning. Instead, he executed a sharp right turn and marched to the office with me following behind, like a tugboat in the wake of the *Titanic*. What transpired in the office was as predictable as it was traditional and would, years later, inspire a confessional poem called "The Strap."

I mention this incident because it was instructive for both of us. Violence brought us together. Not exactly the Stockholm Syndrome. Jimmy Bunn did not fall in love with his captor; but, pedagogy having failed to impress, my aggression had somehow earned his respect. And my shame at having resorted to the strap, combined with my respect for this young man taking his punishment, when he could have knocked me for a loop, produced a bond of affection between us that has no rational explanation. Proof of this came months later, when I heard a truck stop outside my subsidized school-board housing, boots on the stairs. Then the door burst open, and Jimmy Bunn stood in the doorway larger than life. He was there not to exact a belated revenge but to ask for help locating a cow, pregnant and overdue, which had taken refuge in the bush. As I headed off on a fateful mission with my erstwhile adversary, I took a mournful look at my overcooked and half-eaten round steak on the plate and went in search of its origins.

JIMMY'S PLACE

We found the cow in a grove below the road,
leaning against an alder for support,
her udder swollen, her breath ragged and grating
as a rasp. I could have drowned
in the liquid eye she turned to me.
Her calf, though dead, was perfectly positioned,
forelegs and head protruding from the flaming ring
of vulva. Too large, perhaps, or hind legs
broken through the sac, dispersing fluids.
Much as we tried we couldn't pry it loose
and the flesh around the legs began to give
from pressure on the rope. The cow
had no more strength and staggered back
each time we pulled. Tie her to the tree,
I said, being the schoolmaster and thinking
myself obliged to have an answer, even here
on the High Road, five miles south of town
where the island bunched in the jumble
of its origins. It was coming, by God,
I swear it, this scrub roan with her shadow self
extending out behind, going in both directions
like a '52 Studebaker, coming by inches
and our feet slipping in the mud and shit
and wet grass. She raised her head and tried
to see what madness we'd concocted in her wake,
emitted a tearing gunny-sack groan,
and her liquid eye ebbed back to perfect white.

I came to love Texada and its people. I spent a lot of time knocking about its
rocky shoreline, gathering driftwood, mostly juniper, to shape into bowls and
cribbage boards in the school's woodworking shop. I wiled away many fine
hours, when I wasn't sweating over lesson plans or trying to learn how to

drink alcohol and talk politics, in the presence of Jack Leslie, an old logger and union organizer known to some of the locals as the Hermit of Blubber Bay. Self-educated, well-read and sharp as a tack, he had not only fashioned his cozy shack from driftwood but also crafted exquisite models of famous sailing ships. His wisdom and patience as a mentor, combined with his delectable home-made dandelion wine, contributed significantly to my re-education. It couldn't have been easy, for my ignorance seemed as vast as the ocean lapping at the rocky shore outside his cabin.

Fortunately, we had a mole in Westview who let us know whenever the school inspector was catching the ferry to Texada. As the news spread from one classroom to the next, serious transformations took place. I quickly dispatched one of my students to fetch the guitar from my apartment, so when the inspector made the rounds, he found the entire class singing along with me to a hasty and clumsy translation of Pete Seeger's "Where Have All the Flowers Gone?"—*Où sont allées toutes les fleurs, il y a longtemps?* The inspector was so impressed, he would later ask me to head the French Department at the high school in Westview. Fortunately for those students, and for the future of the French language in B.C., I had the good sense to say no. I had other plans, including a postgraduate diploma in education on a slightly larger cluster of islands known as Great Britain.

Valdy's observation that islands are differences of opinion surrounded by water may have become a cliché, but that's all the more reason to take it seriously. I have found that islands also have a way of accommodating, perhaps even resolving, many of those differences. Because there are so few of us, we depend on each other in emergencies, big and small. Ideologies aside, we recycle vigorously, shop for busy friends, provide meals for disabled neighbours, keep watch on properties whose owners are on holiday or visiting family. But islands are always changing. The iron mine at Gilles Bay swallowed one of my students; local roads took the lives of a few others; and the limestone cancer at Blubber Bay continues to eat away the north end of the island. Adjustments are continually required, but this becomes easier as you learn to love and adjust to the constantly changing weather and tides in this dramatic intersection of water, earth and air, along with the shifting tectonic plates and opinions among neighbours, friends and myself.

My main discovery on Texada is that you don't go to an island to teach; you go there to learn.

KATHERINE PALMER GORDON

GABRIOLA ISLAND

LOVE, SURROUNDED BY WATER

"You know what the definition of an island is, right?" teased an acquaintance when I told her I had moved to Gabriola Island. She savoured her punchline for a few moments. "An argument surrounded by water!" she finally exclaimed, grinning broadly.

I laughed dutifully. I'd heard that joke several times already by then—it was originally coined by musician Valdy, referring to Salt Spring Island as "a difference of opinion surrounded by water"—but I had to admit that it applied equally to Gabriola. It hadn't taken long to learn that the island was a hotbed of contention over various burning issues, both large and small. It had been that way for eons before I arrived in late 2003, in all likelihood, since human beings first set foot on its rocky shores and decided to stay.

At the time I was settling into my new home, my fellow islanders were embroiled in the tense run-up to a referendum on incorporation scheduled to take place the following spring. During my first few months on the island, it seemed to be the main topic of conversation at every dinner table, with opinion sharply divided over the merits of staying part of the Islands Trust and the Regional District of Nanaimo or swapping them for our own island-based municipality.

An overwhelming vote against incorporation eventually put that squabble firmly to bed. It was quickly replaced, however, by various spats over the regulation of holiday rentals, a proposal to paint the island's power poles with arty designs, the rules for home-based occupations, the building of a community-owned medical clinic, setting up a bus system and horse droppings on the walking trails, among countless other things. You name it, and Gabriolans seem to have fought over it.

I quickly became as involved in all the issues as everyone else. More circumspect than some, I nonetheless didn't hesitate to make my views clear. Sometimes I chose the side of change for what I saw as the better; at other times I was adamantly opposed to ideas that would alter my new home. In other words, I had become an islander through and through, diving into every issue with gusto.

Outsiders could be forgiven, then, for seeing Gabriola as a sea-bound landscape of never-ending arguments, an island plagued by polarized opinion and irreconcilable feuds. But consider the issues more carefully, listen closely to what people are saying, and something quite different rises to the surface of the conversation. Underlying all the disputes and dissent is this simple but fundamental characteristic that islanders all have in common: we care about Gabriola and what happens to it. We quarrel furiously, we send irate letters to the editor of the local paper protesting opposing opinions, the shouting at contentious local Islands Trust meetings sometimes drowns out appeals for order, and the social media community pages are constantly on fire with clashing views, but tune out the discord, and what you hear instead is simply this: "I love this island."

Something I love about living on Gabriola is taking the ferry to Nanaimo, despite the long waits to board at peak sailing times. Lining up early offers me the chance to go for a stroll, lean in the window of an acquaintance's car and chat about matters occupying us on the island: the lack of rain to fill the wells and cisterns, the power outage last Sunday that ruined dinner, the new café opening up in the village—would this one finally succeed where all its predecessors had failed?

It is also an opportunity to grizzle about the latest irritation. Isn't it a shame they renamed the White Hart Pub, the new name is awful; those people setting off fireworks during the summer fire ban should be deported to Nanaimo; there are too many tourists this year, you can't get a parking spot at the village on Saturdays for love or money; how about that new mall development that's proposed down from the village? That's not going to help with anything.

When I first moved to Gabriola, the island's central shopping hub, called Folklife Village, was just a little nucleus of shops including the grocery store, the pharmacy, a realtor's office and the library. Directly across the road, a small and awkward plaza with virulent green plastic awnings housed the bank, a doctor's office and a dentist, the insurance agent and an optometrist. Now there are also two new state-of-the-art West Coast-style malls just down the road. The buildings are all fashionable corrugated steel and cedar siding, featuring an Italian restaurant, a café, a boutique jewellery store, a health food outlet, a deli, an architect's office, an outdoor clothing store, a large home goods depot, a hairdresser and even a commercial gym.

Initially, islanders really struggled with that development. The predictions of doom and gloom while the malls were being built were dire. The island businesses can't take more competition, and they'll be forced to close! No one will shop at the new malls, and we'll be left with a bunch of derelict buildings! Next thing you know, there will be a McDonald's here! Happily, none of these predictions came true. No fast-food outlets have raised their flags on our shores, and all the businesses, both new and old, are well-patronized by tourists and locals alike.

But at least that debate wasn't particularly contentious. It isn't always that way. Gabriola is a small island, and sometimes the arguments can be brutal. The passion with which we fight for our respective causes can come out in eye-watering epithets and rudeness, in rank accusations maligning each other's intelligence, competency and maturity, even—according to local folklore—in sugar in certain gas tanks.

This type of contention is normal in any community, of course, but it is disproportionately magnified in the fishbowl of a small one from which there are only two main exits: the ferry at the north end or the floatplane at the south end. I can't help but think there must be people out there who have to abruptly reverse direction when they accidentally turn into the same aisle in the grocery store at the same time.

The bridge debate that took place a few years ago divided islanders along two simple lines: either we desperately wanted a bridge to replace the overloaded ferry system, or we feared the drastic changes to our island that would result, and were vehemently opposed. That elongated war of words lasted more than two years, a mass airing of insults and slurs that rose to a cacophonic crescendo of aggrieved incredulity when the pro-bridge brigade persuaded the provincial government to fund a feasibility study on the subject.

A bridge hasn't been built, and probably never will be; the feasibility study concluded it simply isn't viable. Despite the inconvenience of the ferry, I'm happy about that. After all, notwithstanding all the shouting, being on an island is what unites us. It's the water that surrounds our arguments that defines who we are: islanders, more joined than divided, more caring than unconcerned, more joyful together than miserable in our solitude.

Yes, we fight sometimes, but we also show up en masse at fundraisers for the community hall, for the medical centre, for the arts council, for the family who lost a child, for the woman whose uninsured house burned to the ground with all her possessions. At Halloween, the volunteer fire brigade circumnavigates the island on trucks festooned with coloured lights, collecting donations to the food bank, and holds a one-stop-shop trick-or-treat party at the beach for the kids. On Remembrance Day, the parking lot at the police station is always packed as islanders stand shoulder to shoulder, regardless of their differences, to pay their respects. At Christmas, dozens of volunteers prepare dinner at the community hall for all those who would otherwise be alone that day.

Individually and collectively, we are the sum of this island. And in the end, Gabriolans are far more united in love of this place than anything else. We *are* Gabriola. We are love, surrounded by water.

PETER HAASE

THE SALISH SEA, SALT SPRING ISLAND

IN TOUCH WITH THE SEA

D espite having enjoyed many journeys inland on diverse continents with barren deserts, frozen terrains, rushing rivers or lush tropics, I always have to live by the sea. Breathe the fresh seaweed-scented air. Dip my feet, swim, snorkel, sail and, in the past, scuba dive into the deep, enjoying the shock and chill of the ocean where the other-world silence is interrupted only by bubbles from my regulator, as I cruise among forests of bull kelp, sea anemone and innumerable sea life. Some fish dash away; some smile and watch me. Once, a very large sea lion, the size of a cow, flew past me at a dangerously high speed. A direct hit, and ida binna gonna.

Salt runs through my veins, way back to the River Mersey, the Baltic Sea and my sailing ancestors. From childhood, I've had a passion for the hook-and-line game of catch and release or the catch-and-cook reward in a frying pan. Besides fishing, I just love to relax and gaze at the expanse of the deep cold blue from shore or craft. Imagining and absorbing the mystery beneath that plate-glass or tempestuous surface. Sometimes enduring the tipping and bailing of leaky boats.

I found my lucky strike when I finally arrived on the West Coast of Canada in '72.

In the late '70s, our good friends Cathy and Dwain built a house and settled on Mayne Island, and a year later Mona and I bought a half acre, in Village Bay, to be used as a summer escape with a small camper. Soon afterwards, in '83, we left the madding city of Vancouver, and moved to Beach Grove, Tsawwassen.

There, I got my first sense of the history of the Coast Salish people who'd lived along the coast since time immemorial. Six months before we moved into the old beach cottage on the Mud Bay side of the Tsawwassen Peninsula, a stone axe-head had been unearthed in the very garden where we now planted our potatoes. The neighbour told me the ancient tool now sits in the UBC Museum of Anthropology. The oldest finds in the Delta area date back to 2200 BC and beyond, including an ancient straw shoe found on 16th Ave.

Five years later, working as an electrician installing the main highway lighting to the ferry terminal, I learned that the base of the north bluff had been a continual burial ground for the Coast Salish people for thousands of years. Tsawwassen, an island in ancient times, was home base for these seafaring peoples who ventured out in their large dugout canoes for weeks on end, harvesting, gathering and trading. Now my family and I lived on these historic lands, the start of our drift toward the Gulf Islands themselves. The jewels in the crown.

That first summer out of the city, we spent our honeymoon island-hopping with our old Valiant Slant-Six, carrying a car-topper. We visited Mayne, Galiano, Wise, Salt Spring, Saturna and Pender Islands. At that time, once you had left Vancouver or Victoria, the ferries were free between the Gulf Islands, even with a car, so we enjoyed many days of carefree travel on a limited budget. At East Point Lighthouse on Saturna Island, we cast our fishing lines from the low-lying sandstone rocks, into the rushing tide, and both caught a coho salmon at the same moment. We found the islands and the Salish Sea magical.

During our seven years in the Tsawwassen area, I would take off once in a while with my aluminum boat and old outboard motor to the ferry terminal causeway, a favourite launching area for small crafts. Along this mile-long stretch of wide pebbled beach, many fishing enthusiasts would set up weekend shelters and tend their driftwood fires, boil crabs and fry their fresh-caught fish. My early morning escapes out on the briny in that twelve-foot Lund with its 9.9 hp Mercury were treasured intervals in a busy life with two young children.

Fishing infringements have stiff consequences, so I made sure to carry my valid saltwater fishing licenses for both countries. I'd unload the boat from the roof rack, along with the motor, fishing gear and supplies. Sometimes, if I'd heard that the coho were running or schooling on small feed, I'd head straight east for the Point Roberts bluff, on the U.S. side.

Out in that wee boat, which I'd christened the *Liverpool Lass*, I'd enjoy unexpected and amazing encounters with sea life or dramatic weather changes. The *Lass* was a bit leaky, with worn-out rivets that allowed a gallon an hour of water to seep inboard. I easily bailed it over the side with my scoop (a plastic milk jug cut in half, with the handle left on). Once, a mile out from shore on a hot summer's afternoon, I'd cut the engine and sent down two long lines on a drift mooch. I'd baited the weighted hooks with herring strip and securely set the rods into their holders, port and starboard, with a small clip-on bell on each rod tip. "Ding ding, fish on!"

I finished a can of beer and leaned way back in my seat, tilted my wide-brimmed straw hat over my burning face and fell sound asleep. The sea was flat and silent, no boats or noises anywhere, just the lap, lap, lapping against the hull. A perfect moment to lull off.

I woke to the loud surfacing of three orca whales, too close for comfort, about twenty feet from the side of my wee boat. In the lead, a huge bull killer whale (as they are sometimes called) with a dorsal fin that looked five feet high. He made a loud Boof! as he exhaled a plume of water and mist into the air. He broke the flat water with his massive black-and-white presence, and a huge glaring eye said, "Who are you?" A few feet behind, a large female and smaller youngster surfaced. Boom! Boom! Blip!

We made eye contact. Mammal to mammal.

They sank and lifted one more time near the boat and then continued. Fifty feet ahead, they turned a sharp left and calmly carried on northward up the strait, rising, blasting plumes of air and diving off into the distance. Foolishly, I had been using my life jacket as a pillow, so I was grateful none of them had given me a gentle nudge and tipped my boat, sending me into the chilly briny.

During my nod in slumberland, the *Lass* had drifted way out into a sea now enveloped in a misty summer haze, which greatly obscured my view of the distant low-lying headlands of Point Roberts and the higher dark band of Tsawwassen beyond. Now, with my "cross-my-fingers outboard," the duty of the moment was to pump the gas, set the choke and pull the starting cord. After a few attempts, it was fortunately "Weigh, hey and up she rises early in the morning." An hour later and low on gas, my spluttering engine finally got me home. I had a decent catch, enough for a golden nugget, fish and chips dinner for four, and an amazing tale to tell my kids and future grandkids. A day to remember.

In 1990, we finally decided to leave the mainland and suburban living for good, and after several positive and fortuitous trips to Salt Spring island, it became the wonderful settling ground for our family.

My fishing and Salish Sea adventures continued, with Salt Spring now the setting-off point. One cool spring morning in '93, offshore a quarter mile from

South Pender Island, I sat with my friend Erik, on his twenty-five-foot double-ender wooden work boat. We sighted two humpback whales a hundred yards away, surfacing and rounding up a large school of herring, which were forming a few wide and boiling herring-balls at the surface. We cut the putt-putt engine and silently drifted on a current toward the rolling mammals. A thick blanket of morning fog stood ten feet above the water, covering the ocean as far as one could see.

"I want to cast into that herring-ball." I called to Erik over the dinning gulls.

"Just for a bit," he said, "and then we back out. Man, just look at the size of those guys."

With the engine turned off, our capability for steering stopped, and we began to slowly spin in tight circles. The magical morning further opened up when the sun awakened over Mt. Baker, turning the dense fog a beautiful pink and orange. Hundreds of rose-tinted gulls circled overhead, screaming, diving and plundering their epicurean feast. Now we noticed those familiar silver-shadow ghosts darting through the whole watery playground. The attentive and opportunistic coho were hungry and active. My rod and spinning reel at the ready, I sent out a long cast with my favourite lure, a four-inch pink-and-white Buzz Bomb, with a sharp treble hook attached. Across the surfacing herring, the slice of painted lead sailed and sank. Hit, hit, hit. Three six-pound coho caught in a dozen casts. Triplets. Ten minutes of fishing alongside the surfacing and sounding of two magnificent leviathans!

My touch with this Salish Sea has given me insight into what may have been common experiences for the First Peoples of this coast for thousands of years. Not long ago, the number of whales, salmon and all other sea life was immeasurable compared to today's figures. The First Peoples' creative ingenuity, survival skills and techniques were remarkable, and their descendants' interconnection to this natural environment is still unbroken. The gift of living on the islands has deepened my respect for this special and endangered ecosystem. We are the voices for her fish, mammal and bird populations, for her complex and delicate coastlines, for her cleansing ebb and flow.

AMANDA HALE

HORNBY ISLAND

FINDING TRUE NORTH

True North is the internal compass that guides you through life. It represents who you are as a human being at your deepest level. It is your orienting point—your fixed point in a spinning world.

Everything is new. I walk in a light morning rain across the contours of Grassy Point where land meets sea, pulsing beneath a new skin of moss-green—underpainting for grass that will come in spring, will darken and turn to gold under the fierce sun of a summer drought. Nature is confounded by this unaccustomed winter warmth, punctuated by the usual storms, but with air so balmy it welcomes birds and lures out-of-season buds. We are at odds, blooming in winter, dying in summer. But from my perspective, I am home as never before, reconciled with the island, aware of the vitality of placement.

I was drawn here in the summer of 1987 after seeing a production of *The Tempest* in Toronto's High Park, set in the imagined Queen Charlotte Islands archipelago, known today as Haida Gwaii. That, together with a *National Geographic* article, an invitation from a friend to camp on her land and a longing to be by the sea, set my course for the Summer of Harmonic Convergence.

August 16-17 of that year saw the world's first globally synchronized gatherings in meditation, coinciding with an exceptional planetary alignment in the solar system. Sun, moon and six of the eight planets were aligned in a configuration called a grand trine—not that rare in itself, but to create a synchronized world event around one was remarkable, and we were part of it. The Gathering on Hornby Island's Healing Land was my introduction to the people who would enter my dreamworld and populate it for years to come.

We formed a circle, islanders and visitors; for me it was an imprinting of new faces and energies that from then on would mysteriously inhabit my dreams, though it would be two years before I moved to the island, and even then I resisted aligning myself, because of what I carried within me—the shame of my father's suicide and the legacy of damage from our family's WWII experience. When you carry unresolved darkness, you are drawn to similar energy. It exists everywhere, even in vacation resorts.

Hornby Island has had many names—the Pentlatch called it *Ja-dai-aich* or Outer Island; the Spanish renamed it *Isla de Lerena*; the British called it after Rear Admiral Phipps Hornby; now it is "Hawaii of the North," according to the internet. I have not changed my name since moving here, though many do, seeking personal transformation on this "magic isle," like Shakespeare's tempestuous island of transformation.

Though I am an island resident, I roam—immigrant, traveller, always coming and going to Toronto, Cuba, Guatemala, my birthplace in England— and wherever I go, I encounter Hornby islanders, or people who have heard of Hornby, who know people that live or vacation here. I love meeting islanders away; the off-island contact spins us around so that we see new facets of each other. Often it is only in the wider world that we connect and realize the commonality we take for granted. We have a reputation; I once was recognized in Toronto as a Hornby islander by the distinctive earrings I wore, made by an island silversmith.

I never lived anywhere this long. I have seen children born, grow, reach maturity and bear their own children—a rare continuity in a place I have never quite embraced. I left home at sixteen and kept moving on, further west, because I am a writer, a seeker, an adventurer—my place on the outside of the circle looking in. Because of my own peculiarities, I have resisted aligning myself with the island culture. Hornby was settled by pacifists, Vietnam draft evaders with a reputation as hippies from the 1960s culture of love and peace. Thirty years ago, I was ready for neither love nor peace. These are blessings of age in my case, all my life a coming to terms, a reconciliation with England, with Canada and now with myself in relation to this specific place.

I have settled on a very particular half acre as it turns out—though at the time of my decision, it was the only affordable place to get me out of the Hornby shuffle of winter rentals interrupted by seasonal scrambling for a private campsite, a caravan or even the back of a camper when the Summer People arrived—welcomed and tolerated for their consumerism. Our annual influx of holidaymakers fills the B & Bs, the rental properties, the campsites and Sea Breeze Lodge—host for weddings and the only "hotel" in town. Summertime is Hornby's kick at the cultural and economic diversity can. While visitors of all stripes vacation, we work—selling stuff at the market, doing the changeover for weekly rentals, cooking, cleaning, harvesting. Come Labor Day, we heave a collective sigh of relief and return to business as usual.

This half acre has given me a grounding pad; space to dig in the compost pile of my life, connecting with my own dark energies, encouraged by a surprisingly specific placement. My father was a member of Oswald Mosley's British Union of Fascists, and as such was interned during WWII, and subsequently threw himself from the Mersey steamer and was decapitated by the paddles. In this house—which was my art studio until I started writing again in the mid 90s—I have sought to recreate my father's head, with handmade paper and seaweed stretched and dried like mummified skin on an armature of wire, inscribed in blood writing with a poetry of longing for my absent father.

As I write I face east, toward the woodshed built by a Denman Island man who died in a car accident long ago; the shed was once filled with wood split on my back porch by a Haitian man who took his own life. When I moved onto this half acre, I was surrounded by potential suicides, all male, a fact that revealed itself gradually over the years as they left one by one.

On a Friday night some years ago, the man next-door shot himself. I was on the phone, facing east to his house beyond the woodshed. A single shot rang out. I thought nothing of it. We often hear gunshots in deer-hunting season. A man living up the hill one block south had been found dead in his house shortly before I moved into mine, the boy in the cabin to the west asphyxiated himself, and a broken-hearted man to the north gave himself to the Salish Sea. I was pinned on all sides. There was no escaping the darkness, I thought at the time, haunted and resistant, though now my placement is revealed as a natural alignment for one who carried her own unresolved dark energies like a magnet—your being attracts your life.

In this house, I have come to terms with my father's absence, and with my alienation from this extraordinary island community so full of love and light and darkness. Nature is a mirror—it only reflects back to us who we are, all our feelings subjective. My own experience has been one of darkness and struggle in this very particular location. How can I believe in coincidence or arbitrary choice as I walk Grassy Point feeling the contours of the land pulsing beneath me? Hornby Island continues to be a vital part of my destiny for this late phase in my life—west, the final direction, where the sun sets—the end of life, the place of descent.

I have transformed my half acre of boggy wetland covered in alders into a garden filled with roses and rhododendrons, irrigated by a pond that holds the over-abundance of water, as the heart holds and transforms excess emotion. Mine has been a solitary house, but it has become a haven for many people, including my Guatemalan family of ten who come every summer and pitch their tents in my garden, revelling in the beauty of it.

Many of the plants and shrubs that flourish here originated in cuttings from friends now dead—Hilary Brown's bamboo and japonica, Muriel Rogers' lilac, Jean Woodley's coral bells, Gerd's mock orange cutting rescued from the labyrinth at the Festival of Myth, now grown into a tall tree branching out each summer into fragrant blossom. I have an insatiable curiosity about the mystery into which these people have disappeared. What is the Afterlife but an allowing of our dead to live through us, in dreams, and as memory—our own distillation of the overwhelming moments of lived experience that we call reality?

What draws us here to this floating rock that began as molten lava south of the equator 350 million years ago and travelled north on the back of the Pacific Plate, reaching the latitude of present-day Mexico about 170 million years ago? What has united or reunited us to share in the mystery of our presence here? After the receding seas began to reveal this island, vegetation sprouted and, approximately 14,000 years ago, coastal Indigenous People began to populate the islands. These are facts, one facet of an astonishing and impenetrable mystery. Are we a community of souls seeking each other out, regrouping from some previous encounters in other lives or dimensions—"how lovely to see you again"—something strange, but magnetic, familiar? Is our jostling together on this rock coincidental; is it reunion or happenstance? Why are we here, and who are these neighbors on our streets?

Mary Fletcher—who renamed herself Olivia and published in 1989 a geological biography of Hornby Island called *Hammerstone*—likened our island community to a wheel that spun. When it stopped, friendships formed and flourished in the pause, then the wheel would spin again and new alliances would be forged with each pause. But no connection was ever broken, she said, for the wheel would continue to spin so that those people from the past would come around again and again. The links are never broken, only stretched. This vision holds multiple possibilities: we may reconnect after a decade; we may meet after another life lived together; we might gaze at a multitude of stars on a clear night and be reminded of each other.

My relationship to Hornby Island has been governed by my life's task of coming to terms with my father's politics and suicide, the weight of it holding me off-kilter. But that weight has driven me through a labyrinth of darkness to a place of power, in alignment finally with the island that has hosted my transformation. I unerringly situated myself surrounded by suicides, attuned to the dark energies of an idyllic place; I reclaimed the memory of an unconditional love for my absent father, who was a hat manufacturer, through a body of sculptural work, constructing his lost head and displaying it at the Community Hall; I have written the WWII story of my family and called it *Mad Hatter*.

I face north, looking across the heart-shaped accumulation of runoff that I call a pond. It drains through my garden, irrigating the roses as it flows toward the roadside ditch. Across that road, beyond the waterfront properties, is the Salish Sea. I glimpse its stormy whitecaps from the upstairs window; I hear the sealions barking in the night, the slapping of their flippers on the water.

North—I turn in a circle—east, south, west and home to true north with arms outstretched to embrace the power that holds me here, no longer resistant.

DIANA HAYES

THE SALISH SEA

I WAS NEVER A SAILOR

Midway to Clallam Bay and well along
Swiftsure's first leg of the race
tetchy wind rising up Juan de Fuca
stationed barefoot on the foredecks
proprioceptive with soft gaze
horizon east between swells
wishing to be finned or waterproof
not two-legged upright and swerving
with no still point to embrace
calling my luck my Queequeg
the helmsman sculling the waves
skipper below tracing graphs
and charts to ply the invisible
stretch that falls before us
watching the paler cast of the crew's
stony faces how the quiet
becomes silence in the receding
calm eerie in the light of day
everyone craving ginger pastilles
only *Picante*'s skipper in his element
dancing the galley solo
with an appetite for ten
our yacht's master in the V-berth
trying to harness his sea legs and me
gripping the cold with tattooed feet
I was never a sailor but fixed
on the silent Morse I beamed
from my temples saying
this is the life it will lift me
stir an appetite for more weather less sail

THE SILVERED BARN

From the back seat of our family's '37 Ford V8, while we travelled down from the Comox Valley on what is now the "old" Vancouver Island highway, I was intrigued by the long, low island a few hundred yards to our left—the forested hills, a few buildings facing us along the coastline and, most notably, a large barn flanked by hay fields, with a fringe of forest along the crest of the hill behind it. Like many barns in the area, this one had a steep cedar-shake roof and unpainted walls the silver-grey of weathered Douglas-fir boards. "Piercy farm," my father would say.

How did he know this?

When he was a youngster on the family farm in Merville, he and a Piercy son were sent to Vancouver to judge pigs at the PNE. Apparently, because they had been raised in rural parts of the Comox Valley, they were considered to be experts on barnyard animals. But pigs? This was an opportunity for us to make faces and swallow laughter in the back seat of the car. Why would anyone cross the strait in order to compare one pig with another? Was it something like a beauty contest? Was one pig not much like another? On our Merville farm, we were more interested in our milk-producing Jersey cows than with the occasional hog grunting and rooting in the mud of its pen.

At the time, I assumed that someone my age on Denman Island must have been living a life similar to mine. We did not think of it as a holiday island. It might have been simply a large piece of the rural Comox Valley that had broken off and floated a short distance away. After all, when the tide was out, it seemed *almost* possible to walk from the southern tip of the Comox peninsula to the northern tip of Denman.

Denman appeared to be almost entirely rural then: farmhouses, barns, pastures, hayfields and forest. Now, however, all these years later, when I return with our family for a summer holiday, I notice rows of houses that could not have been foreseen in those earlier days. Even so, there are still farms and farmers and hayfields and forests on the island. Denman Island has remained rural.

I have noticed, too, that a newer type of farming has been taking place beneath the water along Denman's western coastline. Here, at lowest tides, it is possible to see that the exposed rocky surface has been reorganized into large distinct "fields" or "plots" for the cultivation of oysters. Occasionally it is possible to see the owners or employees of the oyster leases checking their crops. When the tide has come in, of course, the oysters and the borders of their "fields" have disappeared beneath the waves.

Now, despite the island's increased population, family holidays spent on Denman still provide a happy balance between its rural nature (long winding roads, fields of hay, stretches of dense forest, lakes tucked out of sight in the central woods) and the small cluster of shops and houses near the General Store. This large building with its gas pumps and verandah and large front window may not have changed in appearance since its beginning in 1908. For a moment you might think you are in rural Mississippi, but if you step inside the store, you may meet true islanders working behind the counter or simply chatting. You may even meet the proprietor, Daryl himself.

Nearby, between the Store and the small museum and art gallery, the few small shops sell books, cards, hardware and locally produced pottery. Sometimes a restaurant will appear where there had been another sort of business the year before. The following year it, too, may have disappeared.

The large library/community hall is the venue for an annual Writers Festival, bringing authors and their books from as near as Hornby Island and as far away as Toronto—often from other countries as well. High-profile musicians sometimes travel long distances to perform here, knowing they will get an appreciative audience.

One of the central businesses is a realtor who hopes you won't leave the island without purchasing a piece of Denman for yourself.

For visitors and residents alike, it seems important to visit the Saturday morning market on the grounds of the abandoned schoolhouse halfway across the island. While islanders noisily deliver their empty bottles and cans to the recycling shed, you can wander amongst the outdoor stalls where you might find gifts for your friends and relatives, or for yourself: costume jewellery, wood carvings, aprons, knitted hats, bottled preserves, paintings by local artists, fresh vegetables from someone's garden, starter plants to be added to your garden plot at home. Occasionally it is even possible to purchase young trees for your orchard. A supply of free used books can be found in the school's above-ground basement.

Unless a cougar has recently swum across from Vancouver Island to escape the hunters' guns or to search for pets to eat, the only real danger on Denman is the increased traffic when the cars released from the Hornby Island ferry are racing east-to-west across Denman to reach the ferry to Vancouver Island before it fills up or leaves without them. Of course, a parade of cars just off this ferry will soon be racing in the opposite direction.

When planning to leave Denman for Vancouver Island and other parts of the world, it is important to remember that you cannot know how many cars will be waiting in line for the ferry—unless you have phoned ahead to friends in that part of the island, asking them to walk down the steep slope to count them. There have been many times when the waiting cars have not only filled the official waiting area but sit idle in a row up the slope and sometimes as far as the Store.

Fortunately, during the summer months, if the traffic is heavy enough, the ferry may abandon its schedule in order to make the crossing a nearly continuous back-and-forth business—though this is not something a traveller should count on.

For our family—and no doubt for other visitors holidaying on Denman—much of the island has the irresistible pull you might feel from a large and intriguing and beautiful provincial park. We may spend one afternoon swimming in the ocean at Fillongley Park on the east coast, followed by a rigorous game of bocce or croquet on the grassy area hidden within the nearby woods. The other *must* for us is a walk on the well-kept trail that leaves the parking lot at the south end of the east road and takes you down through woods to Boyle Point at the southernmost tip of the island. There, from the edge of a cliff high above the ocean, we can look out upon a lighthouse and the long eastern coastline of Vancouver Island.

Those who prefer to swim in freshwater rather than in the salty ocean will choose to drive the short distance inland to Graham Lake.

While there is still a good deal of surviving forest on Denman, there are small farms on nearly every road, and clusters of houses here and there, but neither the farms nor the houses have dominated any part of the island to the point of making it appear heavily populated. Some strips of land have been sold in small lots for homes to be built, but a number of the old-time farms are still intact. The visitor may discover the studios and shops of various artists down one road or another—some just a few steps from the car, others requiring you to follow a trail deep into the woods before coming upon a gallery half-hidden within an arbutus grove or a stand of Douglas-fir.

To walk down a trail through the woods, to drive north into the mysteriously unpopulated part of the island, to buy a living plant at the Saturday market or to spend an afternoon on the beach, an hour playing bocce and a few minutes chatting in the General Store—all of these contribute to the mystery, beauty and variety that may inspire a visitor to plan an early return to this long low island with its coastline houses, its fringe of forested hills and that weather-beaten barn still standing in the midst of its fields of hay. And to remember riding in the back seat of a '37 Ford driven by a father who once was a boy who accompanied a Denman Island friend to the mainland in order to judge other young farmers' pigs.

CORNELIA HOOGLAND

HORNBY ISLAND

NATURAL HISTORY

Moon rise. A neighbouring island
hoists its hairy rump out of the sea.

A large beast the ocean no longer
has room for. Land brought to its

knees. Pricks of light on either side
of its flank. Auden said that there are

twenty-seven barns in Frost's collected poems.
Twenty-one of them are abandoned,

nineteen are at night. Ruthless things
emptied of their purpose.

These islands, for instance:
all that overburden lying heavy

as cows in a field before rain,
but not useful like cows.

Cloud covers the moon. Dusty
blur of lights—a distant town like the one

Frost outwalked (his word).
Water in a rush

over my boots—some upset
with the road; the creek swerves.

A fawn, months old, dying,
a trickle of blood from its ear.

I lift my wind-up lantern.
Distended belly inches up—

collapses.
      Out here,

rising and falling slide
into darkness.

STEPHEN HUME

SATURNA ISLAND, LUMMI ISLAND, SAN JUAN ISLANDS

PALIMPSEST

The sunburnt outcrops of British Columbia's southernmost Gulf Islands spill across the Salish Sea like tawny beads from a broken necklace of amber. These islands, more than fifty of them with their stunted oaks, peeling arbutus groves, drifts of chocolate lilies and occasional stands of 800-year-old Douglas-fir, all punctuated by the blinding white surprise of hidden shell beaches, shape a curious combination of austerity and richness, the eccentric laid over the archetypal. They range from surf-ringed islets that submerge on a high tide to Saturna Island's Mount Warburton Pike from which one may look down on swirling riptides and the shining backs of eagles, joy-riding summer thermals.

Most British Columbians know Salt Spring, Galiano, the Penders and Mayne with their 15,000 residents, all served by ferry routes that have carried almost 175 million passengers among them over the last fifteen years. Yet Saturna, a scant twelve kilometres off the main ferry route, population 350, remains largely unkempt and incognito despite its Canada Day lamb barbecue and the lesser-known fall pig roast put on as a fundraiser for the volunteer fire department.

From Saturna, the dazzling, two-kilometre-high barrier of the glacier-clad Olympic Mountains and the saurian spine of a Vancouver Island draped in its ancient skin of rainforests dominate to the south and west. To the east, the volcanic cone of Mount Baker, the ash from its last great eruption turned up by the mundane work of backhoes. And at night the horizon becomes a glittering tiara, the habitation glow from an immense conurbation—it increases by 300 newcomers every day—sprawling around the Salish Sea from Victoria through Seattle to Greater Vancouver.

Mountains shelter the Salish Sea from fierce Pacific storms but not from bone-chilling rivers of air that descend from continental ice fields in winter. Violent gales spin counter-clockwise from the southeast to render the notion of shelter an illusion. On Saturna, after a big blow, residents along the exposed eastern shore may go days, even weeks, without power. Yet if winter brings lashings of rain and spindrift, summer brings a dearth. The rain shadow forces a near-arid Mediterranean climate. Rainfall on the southern archipelago is sparse—about one-seventh of what it is at Port Renfrew, only 120 kilometres southwest on the far side of Vancouver Island. Wells run dry. And on south-facing slopes, there are clumps of B.C.'s hardy little native cactus, *Opuntia fragilis*, the brittle prickly pear.

Saturna first entered my childhood consciousness looking north from Island View beach on the Saanich Peninsula toward the lion-coloured side of Mount Warburton Pike. It shouldered mysteriously out of Haro Strait and Boundary Pass, towering over the low-lying bulk of San Juan, Stuart and the other American islands that, by the stroke of a German king's pen, were edited out. The one archipelago, in the language of nationalism, became two. Suddenly, there were the Gulf Islands and the San Juans, divided following an armed twelve-year-long standoff between Britain and the United States. The only casualty of the only shot fired in anger in the Pig War was a British hog on San Juan Island, killed by an ornery American homesteader. The pig's summary execution led to garrisons of Royal Marines and the U.S. 9th Infantry, fortifications, warships, 84 guns and 2,600 men. The ridiculous prospect of men dying to defend a pig's honour led Washington and London to ask the German Kaiser to arbitrate. Solomon-like, he awarded half the islands to each party.

Perhaps the arbitrary cartography is fitting. For me, Saturna is less a place defined by maps than it is a series of enigmatic palimpsests, an awareness of otherness, of dimly apprehended revenants, of older narratives that slowly surface through the glossing of history. A palimpsest is a parchment on which a previously erased or obscured text can be read through what's written over it, the old story mysteriously revealing itself behind and underneath the new telling. The names on island maps themselves are a palimpsest. The Salt Spring of this generation was the Saltspring of settlers and before them it was the ĆUÁN of the W̱SÁNEĆ People. The Saturna of settlers was the Saturnina of the Spanish and the TEḴTEḴSEN, "Long nose," of the Tsawout, or SȾÁ,UTW̱ as they call themselves in the decolonization of language.

As a very young man, I once talked with a very old SȾÁ,UTW̱ woman. She told me on which beach the first of her ancestors had landed maybe 4,000 years ago; told me their names; told me how her grandparents, who still spoke only SENĆOŦEN, would take her, as a tiny girl, by dugout canoe through the islands and stop at TEḴTEḴSEN. The journey was to visit relatives on Lummi Island, W̱LEMMI, the mouth of Bellingham Bay on the American mainland. They had moved there from W̱SI,I,KEM—Tseycum Harbour—on the Saanich Peninsula to escape raiding by northern peoples. She emphasized how utterly discombobulating it was when United States Coast Guard patrols began stopping them during Prohibition almost a century ago and her grandparents suddenly discovered that half the family was now living in a foreign country without having had any say in the matter.

That was one history. The palimpsest, the deeper narrative I think she wanted me to discern in her story, was of the journey itself, that meandering territorial progress from an age before settlers and their maps, a seasonal round through a world charted not on paper but in the brain that receded from her and that she feared was lost forever, sinking back into the sediments of time. There were excellent canoe beaches in Lyall Harbour, Narvaez Bay and Fiddlers Cove, the colonial names laid over the autochthonous ones: W̱TEK,KIEM, SNEUES and ŦIȽES. They'd beach their canoe, and she'd help her granny pick wild crab apples here, dig and smoke clams there, hanging out the rings on a stick to dry and to be retrieved on the return journey.

Yet an awareness to another palimpsest, one beneath even the W̱SÁNEĆ story, refreshes itself every time I stand on the sea-sculpted sandstone shelves of East Point in hope of glimpsing the resident killer whales. Their story is grim. Teeming chinook salmon runs on which the whales depend are tattered remnants. The whales are starving. But this is just a fragment of the story. The entire human presence here, both settler and Indigenous, is marginalia. Our presence represents less than 0.001 percent of the time since the sediments of East Point were laid down. The first palimpsest here is of the Late Cretaceous. It emerges from the runic manuscript of geologic time with the fossil glyphs of ammonites and mighty mosasaurs, ichthyosaurs and long-necked plesiosaurs. They once made their own seasonal rounds. Now they are extinct, scattered recollections in the stone. There's another palimpsest of extinction, the image of a whale carved into the sandstone while 20th-century hunters waited to harpoon (first for art, then for science), one of the orcas. Captain George Vancouver's log from June 25, 1792 marvels that whales were spouting in the Salish Sea at every point of the compass. By 1900, but for the orcas, the whales had been slaughtered. Our impoverished inheritance is names: Blubber Bay, Whaleboat Passage and Whaler Bay.

My wife and I bought land on Saturna as a mooring; and an anchor during sojourns in the Arctic, the Prairies, urban canyons and towers of glass. We built a house at S̱K̲EUWEWĆ, "Warming your back," just off the northwest end of Tumbo Channel. I'd take my daughter swimming with the other Saturna children at Russell Beach, an extraordinary place where the brackish plume of the Fraser River slides over the colder deeps. A different kind of palimpsest. The water in which my daughter swam began at the top of Fraser Pass, 500 kilometres to the east and more than two kilometres above sea level. In high summer, off Russell Beach, the water is up to eight degrees warmer than the colder ocean water below the surface.

After a swim, I'd take her to East Point with a stale loaf of bread. She'd feed the raucous seagulls, and we'd watch the parade of ships turning from Haro Strait into Boundary Pass. I once asked her what she thought a giant container ship was carrying. "That's the *U* ship, dad," she said with absolute confidence. "It's full of *U*s." And where might it be taking all those *U*s? "To the word store in Vancouver. That's where people who make books go to buy all their words. You have to have a lot of *U*s to make enough words for everyone!" This, too, offers a palimpsest of Saturna's maritime narrative. Before ferries, island girls would stuff gowns into ditty bags and row their lissome lapstrake boats all day for a naval ball, dance all night, then row home to feed the chickens. And before the girls in their rowboats, there was the Royal Mail canoe speeding urgent correspondence from Fort Victoria to Sapperton up the Fraser River.

The elegant hulls of sea-going dugouts like those of the Tsawout inspired the design of fast clipper ships bringing tea and oranges from China. Ursula Jupp, who wrote about the Salish Sea in the age of sail, remembered those who rose at 2 AM to watch the clipper *Thermopylae* scud past Victoria on June 24, 1891, her sails the area of half a football field, shining in the light of a near-full moon. Yet before the clippers was the little Spanish schooner *Santa Saturnina*, (about eleven metres long with a crew of twenty-two), which visited more than two centuries ago. There's learned dispute over whether the island was first called Saturnina or Saturna by the Spanish. *Santa Saturnina* was herself a palimpsest.

Some argue she was originally the *Northwest America*, constructed at Nootka for merchant captain John Meares and thus the first European ship assembled on the Northwest Coast. The vessel, renamed by the Spanish after being seized in the Nootka Incident, a clash between Spain and Britain whose resolution broadly shaped what's now Canada, left its name, or a contraction of its name, on the island its new owners charted on June 15, 1791.

East Point's skeletal finger points accusingly at Boiling Reef where the windjammer *John Rosenfeld,* still readying its half-hectare of canvas for the winter northeasters, struck while in-tow from Nanaimo to Juan de Fuca Strait. The New England-built barque was described as the finest specimen of marine architecture ever to leave Nanaimo, which it did in February of 1886 carrying the largest shipment of coal yet dispatched from that harbour. After grounding, she couldn't be floated free. The wreck survived long enough for enterprising Saturna salvagers to strip the hulk of useful equipment, running gear, much of the cargo of coal and even the stout planking that they used ashore. Then, in a March gale in 1891, the ship slipped off the reef and vanished in sight of the lighthouse built in 1888. That marine disaster, too, is a palimpsest.

Now the throbbing propellers from her descendants in commerce, the 11,000 large vessels that transit the Salish Sea each year, threaten the whales. The constant noise disrupts echolocation.

The killer whales still cruise past the Saturna in whose sediments the primordial story of their ancestors is written. WSÁNEĆ descendants of families who travelled the Salish Sea in canoes still come to Saturna to exercise the hunting rights that predate colonists. The hulls of their canoes live on in tall ships that visit Vancouver. Comfortable settlers take little notice of the strewn stones once hewn by hand for the province's legislature buildings. The scattered islands of serenity seem adrift in their timeless inland sea, surrounded by seething modernity. The little wild crab apples that once sustained Palaeolithic Tsawout foragers are still gathered for the jams and jellies of newcomers who make their living in cyberspace. Palimpsest upon palimpsest out back of the outback.

CHRISTINA JOHNSON-DEAN

GAMBIER ISLAND

GAMBIER ISLAND ESCAPE

I first packed for my friend's cabin on a remote south-facing point of Gambier Island when my children were four and six. Our kit list was simple: food, drink, bedding, clothes and toiletries. Everything had to be easily portable for walking on the ferry and then taking a water taxi. Fortunately, we no longer needed diapers (nor the hassle of taking soiled ones home since there would be no garbage pickup or washing machines). With two young children who could only manage their small travel bags, I had the challenge of packing the rest in my backpack, a cooler and a grocery box.

When I learned there would be another visitor traveling with me—a graduate student in his twenties—I imagined that he would carry only a backpack, leaving his hands free to help me. Surprise, being from Kerala State in southern India, he was a strict vegetarian and found it imperative to bring not only the familiar rice, lentils, yoghurt and vegetables that he knew and loved but also his pots and other utensils, so that his meals would not be contaminated by our North Americans' meat preparations. It looked like getting to Gambier Island with our boxes and bags was not going to be easy. However, our new friend was not only strong but positive and smart. He had the foresight to bring a wheeled carrier, upon which we stacked our gear and easily rolled it onto the vessels. After paying $20 per person for the water taxi (a big gulp for a foreign grad student and a single-income family), we were on our way. There was no charge for accommodation, so we would be home free!

And it was free. In fact, if we had a million dollars, we couldn't spend it, as no shops, attractions, rides or museums were in any feasible distance from our location on a rustic site surrounded by lapping water, deep forest and stunning mountain peaks. Isolation turned out to be one of Gambier's best features. We arrived at a place with "nada" ways to spend money, yet complete with everything needed to wisely while away summer days.

The usual chores were few. Straighten out your sleeping bag or not—who cared? Dishes? Nope. Water was scarce, so we ate a lot of finger food and used paper plates—we wrote our initials on them for reuse. If it seemed kinda dirty, we just folded it over and used the clean half. When it seemed that sanitation was being stretched a bit, it was time to burn the paper plate in the wood stove. Laundry? Not enough water. Instead of putting on heavy head-to-toe protective gear for activities like motorcycling, I prefer to wear as little as possible in the summer. Nothing is needed if the swimming is at your doorstep. Once in the water, the people passing by in boats can only see your head. But if other visitors and decency require a swimsuit, that's okay. Put it on in the morning, and you are dressed for the day. Well, all right, shorts and a top also work, so you are not too exposed to sun and brambles. Absolutely no fancy party clothes or shoes required. The point is: fewer clothes means less laundry. There are no concerns at our hideaway about archaic decency such as "No shirt, no shoes, no service." More clothes might be needed for keeping warm when the sun goes down and the wind comes up, but dirt does not matter—a smear of ketchup easily disappears in the dark.

On Gambier meals are simple. I can be happy with a bowl of cereal with milk. Many kids agree (even for dinner). Add fruit and you've got basic nutrition covered. We make preparations part of the entertainment: setting the crab or prawn traps, fishing off the dock, hiking to the best berry bushes, making jam if all the berries haven't been gobbled down. It's much more fun to cook and clean up together. Summer means enjoying leisurely meals with long-time friends and new acquaintances, especially people who would never be on one's flight path. As for cooking, my friend has become a chef par excellence with the propane stove and barbecue. Did you know that one can bake pizza, scones and cookies in a barbecue? (Later, on my 65th birthday, she even made me a birthday cake.) On that first trip, we feasted on typical North American summer fare—hamburgers, hot dogs, corn on the cob warmed in moistened husks, fresh crab and shrimp from the sea and were treated to authentic Indian curries. In later years, other visitors would delight my palate with foods from Asia and Europe, as well as unusual delicacies from Canada, like moose steaks. We say that the food tastes better on Gambier, and it always holds true.

Most importantly, Gambier means being outdoors—a walk to the latrine, a stroll along the beach to see what treasures have floated in, or a ramble up and over the forested hill to see what the other island residents are repairing, improving, building, growing, raising, reading and thinking. We find endless entertainment with rowboats, kayaks, dinghies, sailboats, floats, floaties and docks. Old piles from defunct logging activities for tying up booms, wave-blocking contraptions, rocky reefs with seals and watching what goes by: the water taxis, a slick new powerboat (usually kicking up way too much wake) or the weekend kayakers from the next bay over. For me, the kayaks on Gambier hold irresistible allure—balanced on logs only a few steps away from the beach with no special car racks or wheels required, no arranging a companion's available time, no overcrowded beach access and limited parking spaces. Instant fun. Simply lift kayak over rocks and plop in water.

So what else do we happily and enthusiastically do all day without spending money? The key is the water. Yes, a shortage of fresh water on this dry point of land constricts our usual cavalier use, but the sea expands our lives with always astonishing wealth. Number one for me: swimming in clear, surprisingly warm and not very salty seawater. I can return from a week on Gambier without having a freshwater shower and think nothing of it. What's so perennially intriguing is that the water and the shore continually vary from early morning glints of light to the full solar flush of day, then evening shafts of sunset glitter through the trees, and finally, the moon shifts through its twenty-eight-day cycle, dipping and dancing on the sea, slinking behind the coast mountains, playing hide-and-seek with clouds, growing enormous as it rises through haze, dimming the stars when full, or disappearing all together so the sky sparkles with stories and myths. But the most mysterious and magical nocturnal experience happens in the water with dinoflagellates, whose bioluminescence glimmers and flashes when disturbed. My first experience of this phenomenon occurred on Gambier Island. Ecstatically I watched the swirl of light created as my hands moved through the water and splashed droplets forward and skyward. Filled with awe, I became more mindful of how precious it is to live in the moment.

Related to times of the day but not harnessed by it are the tides, the relentless movement in and out, up and down. When the tide is out, one can swim over and wade around rocks, where usually camouflaged sea creatures and plants become exposed, even bright—sea stars, urchins, snails, mussels, clams, crabs, kelp and seaweed galore. In the tide pools and among the stony outcroppings, the movement is eye-catching, especially if it's one of the garter snakes, lounging in the sun and feasting on the scurrying sea lice. Low tide signals the time for treasure hunts among the flotsam and jetsam carried to our patch of pebbly beach from the shores and boats of other island dwellers. It may be a useful plank for building a seaside deck, a bolt or nail that can be straightened for a second life on a chicken coop or garden frame, a plastic shoe that can be mated with a find from another day, a grungy but still floatable life jacket, a long thin log that can serve as a stairway railing or a crooked and polished piece of wood that becomes the perfect cupboard door handle. Sometimes the finds exist as purely beautiful and decorative, the perfect ingredients for craft projects—whole and fragmented shells, glass of green, brown, blue, even red or yellow with edges rounded by waves, as well as stones of myriad colours, lines, patterns. It's never the same—the sea emerges endlessly bountiful and full of surprises.

When the tide comes in, swimming is the most luxurious—warm as it creeps over the sun-blanched rocks, clearer and fresher. It seems contradictory—shouldn't it be pushing all the debris from the ocean floor forward? Maybe there's just more water? Whatever. In the late afternoon, swimming provides the perfect denouement to a day's project. Whether we have been kayaking over to a cove where the old homestead was located, walking through the woods to an abundant salal or huckleberry patch or rowing to another islander's place to compare practical notes on water collection, boat docks, outhouses or generators, a swim brings closure to the day.

A swim is also the quintessential ending to a day of puttering about making stone steps to the beach, stacking wood in the shed, adding curtains to the chicken house window, sorting the emergency supplies of food—jams, pickles, canned meat or fish, boxes of pasta, crackers, tea; rearranging the musty collection of practical nature guide books and decades old paperback fiction; checking the tarp on the hill where we collect water and then clearing the funnel for the pipe to the water tank; digging around in the drought-resistant garden and mending the rustic fence to keep the deer out.

But wait a moment, aren't these chores? I guess so, but somehow on Gambier Island, chores feel entirely different—not boring drudgery that can make one feel guilty if not done immediately, but enjoyable tasks shared good-naturedly with others. True, my friend has done many hefty chores (like lugging in huge propane tanks) at other times, so we visitors are more comfortable. But some jobs are reserved for us, no perfection required, just camaraderie and the sense that something was accomplished. If it's not quite right, we'll fix it tomorrow... or maybe sometime in the future. So a swim later in the day is well-deserved, and I sleep better with the dust of tasks washed away.

As the sun sets on the Salish Sea, I recall a conversation I have had from time to time with my sister. We dream that we lived on this coast before powerboats and take-out pizza, and think of being content with life here, especially in the summer. Yes, there would have been chores, but making cedar-bark clothes, cooking salmon over a fire, gathering berries and plants with friends and family, having time to contemplate the woods, water and sky, without the rush of traffic and pressures to complete paperwork, sounds attractive, even idyllic. Though we guess Indigenous People and early settlers had our same kinds of worries— were they making the right decisions for love and good health, were they doing the right things to survive and stay safe—we suppose that they too sat on these shores, the sustaining water of the sea at their feet, and felt the perfection of a summer day well spent.

DES KENNEDY

DENMAN ISLAND

THE INADVERTENT GENIUS OF
YOUNG LOVE

Back in 1970, when love took control of the story, its form was not a love of islands but of the entrancing young woman I'd just wed. Whatever we imagined our shared future might hold did not consciously include islands. Overworked social workers in Vancouver, yes, we chafed to get out of the city, to be, in the idiom of the day, goin' up-country. Maybe the Chilcotin or Cariboo. Maybe somewhere up the Fraser Valley. Truly clueless, we spent weekends purposefully examining acreages on the Sunshine Coast and Vancouver Island. But no place really seized our hearts and cried, "Yes, this is it!"

Then one Sunday afternoon, meandering south toward Nanaimo after careful consideration of five acres of overpriced swampland in the Comox Valley, on a whim we guided our old VW van onto a miniature ferry and crossed Baynes Sound to Denman Island. Off the ferry and up a steep hill, we came to a tiny village of uncalculated quaintness—a small wooden church and matching little general store, a classic old community hall and a cluster of vintage homes. Straight away you could feel hooks being set. We meandered down narrow country roads past scattered farms with agreeable old homes, weathered barns and split-rail fencing. Past glittering seascapes and extensive tracts of fir and cedar forest. Unmistakably, something whispered to us, "If this ain't it, there probably isn't an it."

Looking back half a century, it's easy to see that some aspect of young love surely was at work here, just as it had been with the winsome young woman with whom, miraculously, I was now partnered. That same sweet cast of beguiling love that youth alone truly knows.

Within weeks we'd purchased eleven acres of woodlands for the considerable sum of 6,500 dollars. As with our solemn "til death do us part" vows the previous autumn, the purchase was made with a trusting reliance on instinct and intuition. Soil type? Sunlight exposure? Available water? Didn't enter our heads. Nor had we bothered to notice that there were no power lines along the tiny dirt road. The beauty of the property, a gentle little valley of big timber and sword ferns through which a merry stream trickled, was paramount. Entrancement with place simply eclipsed dull practical considerations.

Due diligence concerning the community didn't occur to us either. The island might have been crawling with lumpy rednecks or sectarian fundamentalists for all we knew. But it felt otherwise. We sensed a gentleness, a subtle intimacy inhabiting the fields and forests. There were about 250 permanent residents—some descendants of the original settler families alongside retirees who'd arrived during the previous several decades—with a smattering of summer people. An aging population for sure—enrollment at the two-room elementary school had dwindled to fewer than ten students, and the school was on the verge of being closed.

But there was no sense of a Goldsmithian deserted village collapsing into dereliction. Rather an island in waiting, an isle in time.

The deepest human history of the place lay buried in extensive shoreline middens where generations of Indigenous People had gathered food from shore and sea. Calling it The Inner Island, the Pentlatch people had been here in their thousands before the ravages of smallpox. Patches of remnant old-growth forest and mossy railbeds running through younger woodlands told of the early years of big timber logging. Picture-postcard farmsteads whispered memories of planting, harvests and extended family celebrations. Tightly packed with secret life, the island seemed a patient place awaiting what was to come.

Now, inadvertently, Sandy and I, and several friends who joined us for a while, stepped into a new chapter, part of a back-to-the-land incursion that would soon engulf and eventually transform the sleepy little island. What a group. Mostly white, straight, middle-class kids, we turned out to be an eclectic bunch, including workaholic back-to-the-landers, politico/spiritual aspirants as well as trippy hippies. Still, most of us managed to look like generic graduates from Ken Kesey's Merry Band of Pranksters. Fabulously lush beards and wild heads of hair on the men, women more given to bracelets and beads than brassieres. Infants suckling at breast in public places! Little kids in face paint running around naked. Feral-looking dogs. Brazen smoking of marijuana. En masse we presented an audacious affront to a way of life that had obtained on the island for generations.

Imagine the shock to old-timers or genteel retirees to suddenly start encountering blissed-out hippies wandering barefoot down the country roads, furtive draft dodgers skulking in the woods or earnest back-to-the-landers pontificating as though we'd personally invented the growing of vegetables and raising of livestock. "The New People," we were called in politer circles.

If not exactly a clash of civilizations—and certainly insignificant compared to the unlawful displacement of Indigenous occupants barely a century earlier—it was at least a perfect setup for fractiousness. A decade of feisty dustups ensued encompassing nude swimming at the lake, whether or not to allow a preschool for hippie mums too lazy to raise their own kids and landowners' rights to subdivide however they chose. Not everyone was caught up in conflict; many of the old-timers welcomed new blood, and many of us astral travellers appreciated the earthy wisdom of the elders.

Sandy and I spent our first seven years living in a one-room cabin without electricity or running water, an episode that in hindsight we wouldn't trade for a luxury beachfront condo. Determinedly outdoorsy, we cleared by chainsaw, axe and mattock the small corner of the property that had been obtusely clear-cut. We planted and harvested a big vegetable garden, tended goats, chickens, geese and ducks. We wildcrafted mushrooms and berries, stinging nettles and oysters. We inexpertly felled timber and milled wood for a future house and split implausible piles of cedar shakes with mallet and froe. After a day of hard labour, exhausted but gratified, we'd sit at a campfire under fantastically starry, starry nights.

Gradually the island opened itself to us. We came to learn something of the wisdom to be gained from time spent among trees. Digging a fifteen-foot well by hand revealed subterranean secrets of stone and shale and the intricate tricklings of water. Obdurate stumps at which we hacked by mattock and extricated by come-along, or eventually blew out with ill-considered dynamite, proved eloquent instructors concerning strength of purpose.

Years before, the Trappist monk Thomas Merton observed that humility is the necessary avenue to truth, and in our own way, we were gradually discovering that the tutelage of Nature suggests much the same. Be still. Be quiet. Forget your precious self amid the undertones of fungi, hearsay of leaves. Dream night mysteries within the haunting calls of barred owls. The love songs of massed Pacific tree frogs reverberating through spring evenings as though

Earth itself was singing to the universe. Sounds within a silence dense with life where revelations await.

The human community proved equally engaging. In the early days, we so-called new pioneers were laboring away at erecting owner-built homes for which the sole design criterion was that they not even remotely resemble a straight suburban house. A Mongolian yurt, a leaky geodesic dome, a retrofitted chicken coop—all were preferable to the dreaded conformity of suburbia. House-raising bees were pandemic, eventually followed by housewarming parties featuring extravagant potlucks and unbridled consumption of blackberry wine and homegrown dope. Flirtations flourished. Couplings and uncouplings and recouplings occurred with dizzying frequency.

We'd have haying bees as well, with one of our cadre aboard an ancient tractor pulling an equally ancient wagon while we field hands heaved and stacked the bales like rustic worthies straight out of Thomas Hardy.

Oh, and the dances that rocked the old community hall in those days! There'd be chairs lined along the perimeter and the centre jammed with flailing bodies. Doug and the Slugs, Pied Pear and other bands on the hippie circuit squeezed onto the little stage and played long into the night. Halloween dances were especially wild extravaganzas of outlandish costumes and questionable behavior. Little kids would sleep safely on a bed of coats in the corner.

We entertained ourselves with unfettered talent shows, Christmas pageants and local theatre productions. Belly dancing, fire eating, rooster crowing—there was no end of wonders on offer. All through the summer, Sunday afternoons were devoted to softball games with dozens of people in the stands cheering on the locals and chatting through those languid afternoons.

These were the formative days of consciousness-raising women's groups and eventually men's groups on-island. Held feelings were released, often with tears, shocking paranoid fantasies revealed, constructive criticisms tactfully delivered, tricky self-criticisms too and, mercifully by the end, appreciations expressed. To further deepen the human growth potential, itinerant gurus would periodically drift ashore to instruct us on how to Be Here Now á la Baba Ram Dass, how to master the Transcendental Meditation techniques of the Maharishi Mahesh Yogi and, embarrassingly in retrospect, detailed instructions on how to become The Superior Man.

Over the years, we had our share of tragedy too, of course. House fires and accidents. Tormented souls. Abusive relationships. Illness and untimely death. But even during the darker days, we held together through the glue of community. A spirit of selflessness did, and still does, roam the place, manifest in random generosities and unbridled volunteerism. Beneficial committees self-replicate recklessly.

From early days, love of the island segued seamlessly into a collective determination to prevent its ruination. Of necessity, political organizing became a way of island life. We battled unscrupulous logging outfits and shady developers attempting end runs around the community plan and bylaws. We thwarted an ignorant scheme to develop a huge log-booming facility in Baynes Sound and an equally obtuse plan to dump all the Comox Valley's raw sewage close to Denman's northern shores. We formed a community land conservancy that successfully protected key habitats on the island. An early recycling depot and reuseables store, along with a summer farmer's market, formed a bustling social hub. Further afield, we joined with regional peace activists to protest nuclear weaponry at Comox Forces Base and at Nanoose Bay. Denman's seasoned activists played key roles in the civil disobedience campaigns in defense of Strathcona Provincial Park, Clayoquot Sound and other environmental hot spots.

Considerable challenges still face the island. Reckless overdevelopment of the shellfish industry in Baynes Sound threatens to choke us in a sea of plastic debris lapping against industrialized beaches. Summer tourist traffic, particularly to our dear neighbour Hornby, is an escalating menace. New million-dollar show homes continue to miss the point of the place, not to mention the peril of the planet. Affordable housing for working folks remains a challenge. Successive provincial governments still spinelessly decline giving the Islands Trust the substantive powers originally called for in its visionary creation.

Nevertheless, many islanders continue practicing a conserver lifestyle radically at odds with the consumerist frenzy now poisoning the biosphere. Recent years have brought a refreshing new wave of vibrant young characters determined to live outside the mainstream. Some are the offspring of our Woodstock generation, returning after years away. There's a deepened cultural richness as well, manifest in professional performances, festivals and art openings. Farming, raising kids, making music and creating art—here lie the leavening ingredients for the future of the place.

Fifty years on, the guileless young love that first drew us here has aged into a richly textured affection. Love for a place of exceptional beauty and safety and peace. For the great privilege of being gradually enticed into a lifeway orchestrated by the turning of Earth and passing of seasons. For quiet days spent in touching intimacy with other life forms all around us. For the creation of true community, bringing together gifted and eccentric characters, new people and old, learning to coalesce not for personal gain but for the common good, for the sake of the Earth, providing opportunity for those who come after us to perhaps experience one tiny microcosm of what a better world would look like.

MICHAEL KENYON

PENDER ISLAND

FERRY

Step into the ferry terminal where
causality has left its sandals. Step
alone into the bright passenger lounge.

Every Sunday morning through the spring
of 1942, my mother pushed
her bike through the front door and rode out of

Manchester, crossed into West Yorkshire, caught
the ferry from Todmorden to Pender
Island, where the few people she met were

always quite kind and had no idea
there was a war on. She swam at Roe Lake,
away from family, watched by eagles,

and often dozed on the ferry back home,
and the bike ride at dusk through the moors
into the foggy munitions park was

a physical and mental ordeal,
she said, going to work was still new, she
could smell the lake on her skin all next day.

Fifty years later, she and my father
built a house on Pender Island, where Mum
began to quilt time. A water taxi

took her and then him away to die. Ghosts
of the living and ghosts of the dead mix,
bound by the island's coastline. Who spends time

on land cannot cross water. All ferries
are at sea, and islands throng with berm ghosts,
each perfect circle like a headlamp beam.

VISIT TO PENDER, APRIL 15, 2010

Sunrise over Otter Bay and an up
surge of wellbeing due to warm weather
and singing birds. A quick stay on Pender
to buck maple on the scruffy bank in
front of my parents' house, drinking beer first
and tea afterward, then mowing the lawns
and paths around my trailer, soldering
the new valve onto the outside shower,
quaffing a bottle of wine, smoking dope
and going to bed early, waking up
dehydrated, to the taste of water,
to Jung on Nietsche while the sun rises,
two new pens in the mailbox. Then I fill
the shower barrel and have my first-of-
the-season shower, bike to the clinic
and meet R and J for our first session,
acupressure with B, home to watch Hull
get beaten by Burnley, sleep, wake early
to dawn birds and the walk to the ferry.

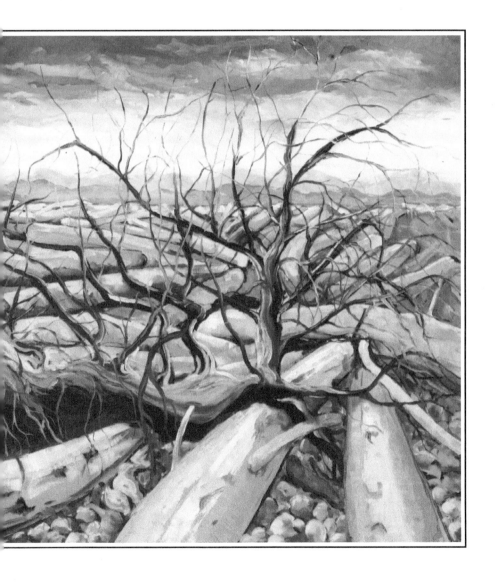

ZOË LANDALE

THE SALISH SEA

LIFELONG

At seventeen, naked, you peer out a porthole
at firs and rock, surrounded by still water, stamped

with reflections, moving. Snowy mountains repeat
north and east. Distant points of land open

down multiple waterways: you're in a Tony Onley print
only coloured like a Japanese fan. You're dazed

with July. Calm sea, the jade whaleback of an island;
the first week of your commercial fishing career.

You are so green you don't know real fishers rise
at four AM. It's now six. So you *Ooo* over the island,

your mouth the mirror of the porthole's brass "O",
ask your red-shirted boyfriend who's been up for half an hour,

has trolling lines in the water, and is, in your estimation, heroic,
beams out knowledge like a lighthouse flashes

every so many seconds, to show you on the chart where you are.
Kinghorn Island. The softness of morning slots you home

in a way you don't understand. Your heart twists like a key
turns in a lock: what just happened? Back at the porthole,

you touch fingertips to lips, blow a kiss to shore, say, *I'm going to learn*
this coast. Wherever I wake up, I'm going to know where I am,

a promise that makes you smile now, close to fifty years later,
for its brashness. At seventeen, did you acknowledge these waters

as your true love (the slow happiness of a body
where it should be) or did the coast claim you first?

Whatever transpired in that substantive instant of give-and-take,
of adoration, you remain open, posture soft,

to green-beckoning headlands,
the coast's glittering world.

PETER LEVITT

SALT SPRING ISLAND

ORCA WEDDING

The sea is all distance, a lover
without end or true horizon,
and yet these waters make a home,
circling rocky coasts and croppings,
the middens of an earlier people
hidden in soft earth beneath the fir and cedar,
the rhythms of their gatherings a continuity
they learned from the seasons and the sea.

My wife and I came to this place late in life,
came to be married and then to live here
and to die among what had always called,
the sounding of currents and waves no different
from a mother who makes the first sound
anyone has heard. It is what binds us together
as surely as the Salish waters bind together
the islands where we make our home.

Our first night, before we would rummage
in the woods to gather the makings of an altar
for the mossy slope where we would say our vows,
I stood outside our small rooms and listened into the dark,
listened to a sound I had never heard before
that lifted from below the cliff edge
in the waters I could not see.

In the morning we sat silent beside our altar,
and looked past the world of no horizon.
Then we said what no one else would hear.
This is when they came,

five of them together. They rose
up out of the waters below us
with the whoosh I heard now for the second time.
"*Yes,*" they sounded—again and again.
Then they made a circle, a perfect ring
to help us seal our vows before they dove
to where they no longer could be heard or seen.

Love has its own way of rising,
letting go or diving deeper still,
though we may never know its root
in the uncertain waters of what we are.
But we came to this place to live as we were able,
and to raise a child who would climb
far beyond our reach in his forest home—
a green-eyed boy who learned the forest's silence,
and took into his body what an island is,
shaped by the rhythms of what can and can't be seen,
in the unbroken lineage of the sea.

DEREK LUNDY

THE SALISH SEA

WATER MAKES ISLANDS

From our islands, our shards of land, we look out at the besieging sea with affectionate and simple gratitude. This is the water that has created our separation, our sense of solitude and sanctuary. We are benignly aware of the picturesque nature of the blue-green-grey sea around us—mirror-calm one day, chopped with whitewater waves the next—but we think of it as an undifferentiated thing: an impassive protective barrier against the outside world, a welcome moat we gladly take time to ferry over to go home. On our beautiful islands, we are the sea's landed benefactors.

Things look different from the other side. From a boat in Salish Sea water, gazing toward the enveloping islands, we experience a kind of field reversal, a flip of perspective. Now it's the sea that seems infinitely variable, absorbing our attention, the green land that presents itself as a blank abstraction and the source of all the sailor's potential hazards. Sailing the Salish Sea is a hard negotiation of water made complex and labyrinthine by its intrusive islands.

Big tides sluice north and south twice a day, twisting through channels, curling around points and capes, doubling back on themselves in confused maelstroms. Where the narrow water is narrowed even more in constricted passes, currents run like rapids. Even when the sea is more or less still, it's cluttered with the land's detritus: fishing gear—crab pot markers mostly—and, always, with logs—floaters and deadheads. The pots can stop a boat dead in the water and entangle its rudder or keel or propeller; a log can eviscerate the boat if it's hit just right. Always there are the land's fringing remnants: shoals, reefs, wayward singular rocks. And heavy traffic: other pleasure boats, tugs lugging barges and log booms, fishing boats single-mindedly following their lines and ignoring the rules of the road, big freighters and ferries that always bear down on you much sooner than you think they will.

In the islands' channels and bays, and in the wider Strait of Georgia itself, the land adulterates the wind, bends it, squeezes its isobars. The high islands sometimes block it entirely; or it rushes down from the high land in gale-force williwaws; it may change direction 180 degrees within a hundred metres. For the sailor, this is a perversion. And when strong wind blows against strong tide, those on the water must take great care: stay put or run for shelter, practice patience—the sailor's most necessary and hard-learned virtue.

The Salish Sea itself is blameless. All these difficulties originate on the land. The open-ocean sailor knows that the greatest hazard is not the stormy sea but the shore. That's what destroys most boats. "When in doubt, go out," is the old, and still-true, adage. It means go out to sea, away from the land, where it's safer, get some sea-room where you can heave to or run off. But in the cramped waters of our inland sea, there's no "out" to go to. The sailor there cannot flee but must find a way to confront and negotiate the difficulties the land presents. The boat must thread her way with caution and cunning amongst the beautiful and dangerous islands.

I bring in my stern shore line and haul up my anchor in tiny Otter Cove on eerie Jedediah Island, nestled between eccentric Lasqueti and big Texada, ex-haven of rum-runners and marijuana farmers. A late-September gale is coming, and I need a better refuge. The wind is building from the southeast—up to twenty knots or so, already a lot of wind for my small boat. Out through cramped Bull Passage under double-reefed main and staysail with the underpowered diesel straining hard too. Tide flooding strong against me, and the boat labours, heeled over onto her rail, pounding into the shallow water's short, steep waves that sluice over the bow and down the windward deck into the cockpit. Low scudding cloud and rain and driving salt spray soak me.

I shut down the engine. We slog our way to windward into the waves and tide, close-hauled into the augmenting wind, right on the nose. In Bull Passage, it's gusty and erratic, then easier as I get out into more open water. For three hours I tack, driving hard across the entrance to Malaspina Strait. I'm seeking the shelter of the Thormanby Islands and the Sechelt Peninsula where I'll be in the lee of the land when the full gale comes.

The islands round about mean nothing to me now, except as purveyors of frustrating, sometimes dangerous, wind shifts and gusts, and of the vicious tidal stream that's pushing me hard toward the shallow water and shoals off Texada. I measure my inching progress against the islands' opaque green and stony shores. I've left their welcome shelter today, and I'm seeking their haven again tonight, but for now, they're nothing but trouble.

On a clear midsummer day, I beat up to the entrance to Porlier Pass between Galiano and Valdes. The pass is one of the few exits from the narrow waters of the islands into the wider expanse of the Strait of Georgia. Tides run through here as strong as ten knots. I'm early, almost two hours before safe slack water, but for no good or seamanlike reason—I'm in a hurry to meet someone somewhere—I decide to press through. The wind is northwest, against the flooding tide that doubles, triples its velocity as the immense moon-driven flow is compressed between the two islands. The water shallows too in the pass, and that amplifies its inexorable compression, creating the chaotic standing waves I can see ahead.

As I dogleg through the 400-metre-wide gap between Virago Rock and Race Point, the boat is mugged by vandal seas, slammed, pounded, thrown on her beam ends, swept by green-grey water. You're a bloody fool, I say to myself. The fast tide is in my favour though, and in a few minutes, the boat sluices out into the open strait, newborn after a tempestuous delivery. The vexatious islands fall away astern, and I sail on over the widening, uncorrupted water.

Beating down Northumberland Channel into a fresh southeast wind and making for Dodd Narrows, where the tidewater current runs so fast I can't chance a transit more than half an hour either side of slack water. There's a big log ahead, then another, and more, big ones, lying low, ten or fifteen-footers but still difficult to see amidst the wind's steep chop. I'm in a field of logs. A boom must have come apart—they line the eastern shore of the channel. I throw the boat into one tack after another to avoid the boat-killing obstacles. No slowing down; I don't have much time to make the narrows. Single-handed as usual, I can't keep up with trimming the sails and sometimes must bear off through 360 degrees to sort things out, then turn to dodge and weave again.

I feel the quickening signs of a sweaty headache, my heart rate getting up there, moist hands on the tiller, ordering myself around as usual when things go awry:

"Shit! Look out! Turn! Dammit!"

I carom off logs, clump over others. Only the boat's brawny bow and long traditional keel prevent damage as they turn aside the timbers or drive them under to slide harmlessly along to pop up astern. Then abruptly I break free, the narrows close ahead, turning against me but still navigable.

Sailing close to home is no guarantee of ease. Less than two nautical miles from my dock on Salt Spring, I'm trying to sail through Captain Passage between the entrance to Long Harbour and Prevost Island. The wind is light from the northwest—the prevailing summer direction—and the ebb tide, squashed into the narrow gap between the two islands, is setting strongly against me. As I enter the passage, the boat stops, lies dead in the water. In reality, I'm still sailing at three-and-a-half knots—my sails are full—but the tide has cancelled my progress. Water runnels by the hull, but when I eyeball trees or rocks on the nearby shores, they stand as still as trees and rocks can. Then, slowly, the boat begins to lose ground. In this ebullient wind, I'm sailing backwards, stalled in the islands' petulant grasp, no love lost between us today.

On yet another summer day, I'm broad reaching along President Channel off the northwest shore of Orcas Island, the fair wind bellying out mainsail and yankee jib. Orcas is one of the San Juans—"their" territory, but it's still part of the archipelago of the Salish Sea. The border means nothing rational in these waters; it's a notion, a conceit, slashing its imaginary, irksome way among the indistinguishable islands.

Ahead of me, I glimpse a sudden eruption of whitewater. Sometimes you *can* see wind. I'm at the mast in five steps, claw down the mainsail and stow it with gaskets. Back to the cockpit just in time to ease the yankee as the williwaws slam down from the high cliffs three-hundred metres away. Even under its reduced sail, the boat heels to the gunwales and accelerates in gusts that must be thirty-five knots or more—gale force. I brace my feet on the low-side cockpit seat and hang on to the tiller; all I can do is wait it out. The GPS shows eight knots of speed. That's a knot faster than this boat can theoretically move, but sometimes, wind and water combine in shamanistic exuberance to slyly sidestep the laws of physics.

The high land of Orcas is intercepting the wind from the southeast, gathering it in, throttling, twisting and jamming it, then hurtling it down its northwest flank, spilling it out onto the water where I'm ambling innocently along. No malice intended; it's just what islands do.

Then there's this.

I clear Pirate Rock at the southern end of Welcome Passage. The wind is on the starboard quarter, the perfect angle for my course to Silva Bay on Gabriola, and it's the ideal strength for the full yankee alone. I set the self-steering wind vane and leave the boat to find her own bustling, knowing way up, over and down the high-running seas. She rolls and twists in the momentary clutch of each swell, surging along close to hull speed.

I slither with care along the windward side—two hands for myself, none required for the ship—and sit on the dry foredeck, braced against the hatch and watch the boat sail herself. Except for the shorter, steeper waves, this is like trade-wind sailing. I feel again the familiar fervent joy of the open ocean—an ecstasy of motion incongruous in these narrow unkempt Salish Sea waters—under the dominion of wind and scurrying broken cloud in warm fitful sun. Moments of consecration.

It ends, of course, as land approaches. I bear down fast on the small reef-littered bay bound by Tugboat, Acorn and the Flat Top Islands off the entrance to Silva Bay. Then it's a fire drill: disconnect and stow the wind vane, furl the yankee, pump out the airlock in the diesel cooling water intake, start the engine, get the anchor ready for deployment, then chug through the dogleg channel into the anchorage, swinging around the rocks that I know extend well beyond their markers.

At anchor in the bay, I'm embraced by the encircling islands' perfect protection. The boat lies on a kind of border, a shifting fringe, where land and sea meet, and I look at both with dispassionate, though ambiguous, admiration. While the boat is at rest, I can discard vigilance and caution, the islands no longer a source of deceit, surprise, treachery. A truce is in effect. That will end when we move again, but for now, we lie in grateful harmony, a temporary reconciliation.

MATSUKI MASUTANI

DENMAN ISLAND

LONG AGO

in a classroom
I heard about
a utopia called
"The Village of Peach Blossoms."

Many of my friends,
even the girls,
soon dismissed this as fantasy.
But I never forgot
the image.

Now
I realize
I am in it.
I am inside that image,
standing in a garden of apple blossoms.

To get here
I left my country,
my city life,
even my career.

I must be nuts.

AT MIDNIGHT

My wife looked out
the bathroom window.
Our fence was on fire.
I'd started it
with wood-stove ashes
I'd carelessly dumped on the compost.

If she hadn't gone
to the washroom,
If she hadn't believed
what she saw—the flames
looked like a trick of the light—
and if our well hadn't had enough water...
It shatters me to think
how many times I have escaped
serious consequences
by chance.

After our fire-fighting,
we saw for the first time
the green of the northern lights
shimmering across the sky,
like a curtain
opening.

KAREN MCLAUGHLIN

THETIS ISLAND

AFTER THE STORM

      sun
behind a thin white cloud cover
lowering halfway down my tall windows

      tide
filling up the cove
half darkened in the shadow of Fraser Point

      eagle
weep-weep-whit-whit-weep-ing
in its nest behind the garage

      white sailboat
jib set, rounds Fraser Point, edges along the far shore

      silver streaks
follow scoters like contrails on the glassy water

      Myrtle
curled up, sleeps outside on a cushioned Adirondack chair

      Canada geese
honk honk honk their way down Cufra Inlet

      moss
lost its luster in the wind, its edges are curling in, browning and crusting

      chainsaw
weekend guy ripping into deadfall a few lots over

the boundary
of light water and dark water zipping and unzipping
as a family of thirteen scoters bunch up and spread apart bunch up
and spread apart

    Bob and Jean
putter about cleaning debris from the traps of their rainwater system

    mast and jib
eye-level, glide past the edge out front surprising me, I
had lost track

    great slabs
of lichen-festooned sandstone outcroppings appear to be
napping after the great scouring

what an uproar in North Cove this week infernal northwest
winds venting a pent-up rage, and we are all
left feeling a little battered
as if there has been a great family fracas

    small outboard
passes from Pilkey Point to Fraser Point creating surface disturbance leaving a
rolling, vectoring pattern in its wake
while deep below, the tide goes about its business inching, inching
inching in

    I
could have made myself busy all day
raking up the thatch of cones and sticks and arbutus leaves but have read
inside, by the window up here on the cliff shamelessly making myself unbusy
unbusy
in the fullness of the day

MAUREEN MOORE

SALT SPRING ISLAND

MY HOME ON SALT SPRING ISLAND

Decades ago, seeking quiet as well as connection with the natural world, I fled a paved municipality and moved to Salt Spring Island. In my old home, traffic noise obliterated birdsong. Municipal road signs that had once warned drivers about deer had been removed as most of the wild animals had left. Trees had vanished in what became an ugly suburbia. It didn't feel like home.

My adult son suggested Salt Spring as a good place he'd once visited. I'll give it six months, I thought. Welcoming me upon my arrival on Salt Spring was the autumn gold of broad-leaf maple trees growing, along with western red cedars and Douglas-firs, at the sides of winding roads. The roads themselves had fanciful names. Sky Valley. Rainbow. Shepherds Hill. Then there were the islanders. Helpful residents gave me challenging directions referencing the island's past, like, "Just turn left where Black Sheep Motors used to be." Within Salt Spring's 182 square kilometers, I became aware that I could explore Garry oak meadows, pockets of lush temperate rainforest, fields, creeks, lakes, mountains and beaches. This island and others in the archipelago contained varied rare plant and animal communities as well as the human population.

One morning, glancing down a ridge toward a nearby storybook lake, the sight of arbutus trees twisting up from rocky soil entranced me. These young trees had smooth reddish bark that glowed in the sun. This unforgettable moment took me by surprise. Arbutus, also called Pacific madrone, is the only broadleaf evergreen tree in Canada, and I'd never seen such trees before. This island offered many such glimpses of beauty, drawing me into a closer relationship with trees and forests. I began to learn to read the land. Salt Spring is in a dry coastal Douglas-fir zone. These firs can live 1,000 years, and if mature, their bark is so thick they can withstand a forest fire. Not every ecosystem on the island is the same. Unlike the arbutus trees I'd seen that need sun and warmth, western redcedars require mist, water and shade.

To be among huge and healthy ancient cedars, I had to walk away from roads until I couldn't hear human sounds. I followed deer paths while sword ferns brushed my legs. Above me the moss-festooned maples glowed green. In fact, broad-leaf maples, the largest maples in Western Canada, hold water in their bark and support the heaviest burden of moss compared to all other trees along the coast. Springing up from these vivid mosses, other plants I saw included licorice fern, the rhizomes of which were used as medicine by Indigenous People. The leaves of these maple trees are so huge, usually bigger than most dinner plates, that the Salt Spring Fall Fair created a contest in which the winner is a child who finds the largest maple leaf.

Under an umbrella of leaves, I wandered into a pocket of rare temperate rainforest where lacy needles clothe the branches of western hemlock trees capable of living for 500 years. When they die, they, like many other trees, provide homes for cavity nesters. Hemlocks are known as the marker trees of the temperate rainforest that exists on only one percent of Earth's surface. In such forests, giant cedars, trunks striped with brown and grey bark, hold out swooping branches. These trees live hundreds of years and can survive a thousand years if they escape logging. For coastal First Nations, cedar was central to life, art and spiritual beliefs.

Indigenous Peoples cut planks and bark from cedars without killing the tree itself. Whole trees were only taken for totem poles or canoes. No wonder coastal First Nations People call it the Tree of Life. Its wood contains a natural fungicide that resists rot. When felled, the remains of a cedar will nurse new life, and it's common to see plants including young hemlocks and salmon berries springing up from a cedar stump.

Within these wet, cool temperate forests, the air is pure, the earth is fragrant and filled with microscopic life. If I remained quiet and unmoving, the forest around me revealed itself. Beneath the leaf litter, rough-backed newts travel quickly as they hide from birds of prey. What had seemed to be part of a tree I now saw was a grey-brown owl. I could hear nature's carpenters, the large pileated woodpeckers, hammering against tree trunks, scattering woodchips below. Red-legged frogs, now endangered, are common in this wet forest habitat where there are usually feeder streams and creeks. Beneath, tree roots share nutrients. These roots communicate with the help of mycorrhizal fungi hidden within an underground web of wood as intricate and interrelated as the visible forest.

The mature cedar I'm sitting beneath may have fused its roots with those of another cedar sending and receiving messages. In a coastal temperate forest, more life exists within the spongy soil than can be seen above, and this invisible world supports the mighty forest. Not only do forests sequester carbon but they also release oxygen. In any forest, a dead tree supports more life than a living tree. In this green world, I felt part of the interconnectedness of what we call nature—as if we are not one with it.

At night, before I slept, I listened to the calls of an owl seeking a mate in spring. The dark was lit only by moonlight. Outside my bedroom window, deer browsed, and I could hear their foraging teeth pulling on grass. Above my skylight, I could see bright stars and the changing moon. "Magical," said Salt Springers, and all this magic came from the generosity of the natural world.

At twilight in the late spring, does curl around their newborn fawns hidden in the lush sword ferns. I learned to move slowly and quietly along the paths they had made. Later I watched mother deer teaching their fawns which trails the family would use, the plants to eat and where to find water. There was an old crab apple tree in my yard, and as soon as the fruit ripened, deer whose routes crossed this way munched on fallen apples. Loyal to their home range and paths, deer are browsers. Adult deer will stand on their back legs to reach a particularly tender leaf. If they feel safe, these gentle ungulates will lie in the sun, curling their delicate legs beneath them while they digest the contents of their divided stomachs.

In summer the bucks regrow their antlers after shedding them every February. Antlers are actually made of bone. Imagine the energy expended to grow this heavy crown every year.

Several generations of deer travel through my unfenced yard. One grandmother doe with a twisted but healed foot didn't make it through a hard winter, but I saw her mature, healthy daughter later appearing proudly with spring fawns. In summer I noticed tourists taking videos and photographs of Salt Spring's deer and recognized the deep human need for connection with wild creatures.

Deer, the natural trail makers, have created the only paths in some forested areas. Once, as I climbed a hill through a woodland with my young granddaughter on my back, I reassured her we were not lost since we were following the deer paths and they knew the right way to reach places above. Our forest journey ended safely at our intended destination, to her relief.

I was present when Salt Spring's Bristol Foster, a naturalist, asked a group of school children if they knew each other's names. "Yes," they responded. "Of course." Smiling, he said that to know the trees, they had to learn their names too. He led them into a forest and introduced them to cedar, hemlock, broad-leaf maple, Douglas-fir and alder.

I began to feel a sense of "belonging," an emotion we associate with home. This was not limited to the shelter of my house. My sense of home now included the towering plants whose names I knew and the wild creatures I saw or heard. Home had expanded to include beaches with tides that moved toward and away from of the island. In late spring, arbutus trees bloom along with cottonwoods, broad-leaf maples and other trees, filling the air with scents. "Nature never did betray the heart that loved her," wrote the poet William Wordsworth, long ago. His words remain true. Nature is generous. Even in winter, just like many other animals, I spent time in a house that kept me warm and dry, but I could clothe myself in my second skin, composed of a coat, hat and boots, required by humans to venture into cold rain.

By now the animals too had grown their thick winter coats. I entered the woods, which glowed jewel-green as trees drank and stored rain, preserving ravines and shading creeks; the forest canopy was my shelter. We are naturally rooted in nature, and if disconnected, we lose a true sense of home for which our spirits long. On Salt Spring Island, with its abundance of beauty, wild creatures and areas of gentle quiet, I feel at home.

ARLEEN PARÉ

MAYNE ISLAND

THE COMMON MERGANSER WINTERS IN DAVID COVE

Last day of the year, mid-morning, the frost-coloured sky
mylars the small cove where a single merganser, singular, male, Common—
though that's a misnomer—floats between the two buoys.
There are people today in the green house on the far shore,
which is not very far. Here for the New Year.
We arrived last night to otter puke on our front step,
pale clumps of unravelled crochet rank
with the rot of raw fish, fish bones and broken pieces of shell.
But the reported dead buck behind the carport had disappeared.
Time offers that kind of magic: right hand, left hand.
This island is all about time—and balance.
An old geological fault near Campbell Bay Road splits the island in two.
Deep time.
If you notice at all. Each year the shining sea rises around us,
not by much, but each year adds up. We live on a mountain.
When I look again, the once black-and-white bird
is no longer there. Common. Though some see the head green.

Arleen Paré

ON THIS SLEEPY GULF ISLAND
After W.S. Merwin's "Thanks"

Listen
with the salt sea rising each year
we say thank you   standing on the shore with baskets of apples
thanking the ocean   cleaning the beach
collecting pop bottles   plastic and glass
styrofoam   old fishing nets
jellyfish saucer the wet sand   red discs in their dead centres
we kneel on the sand   thanking the sand   the salt
thanking the past
and the Pleistocene era   upheavals   mountains sinking
their tops become islands   an oversized puzzle   thanking the Salish
the islands   mountains   the upheavals that fashioned them both

thinking of future   thanking the thought

and the family who lived in our house one hundred years ago
on two hundred acres of farmland   we are thanking the house
thanking the family
forbidden to bury their Catholic father and daughter
in the graveyard beside the Anglican Church
and the mother with one broken hip dislocated in childhood
and eleven small children   thanking them all

and the old man who knocked on our door when we first moved in
saying this once was my house
can I see the upstairs where I slept as a boy
saying thank you   we are saying thank you to him
the king apple tree still stands in the yard   bark weathered and thick
we are thanking the apples   the weather
one hundred years   the old house   the plastic   the tree

140

BRIONY PENN

SALT SPRING ISLAND

OLD LOVE-BY-THE-SALISH-SEA

Finding the first evidence of life—and therefore love in the Salish Sea—took place in the island dump. The dump is a deep, dark pit of crumbling shale that has been mined by islanders to surface their roads with the fossilized evidence of spawning ammonites and clams. Within the black shiny sheaths of shale are the telltale Fibonacci swirls and wave-lapped patterns of mating molluscs whose frolics on our island shores were instantly halted one spring day 70 million years ago by a mudslide.

Daphne and I had taken our twelve young students to uncover the first creatures to crawl upon or at least swim around their island. Rather than Jesus and the Holy Spirit sermonizing creation from the mount, we two island gals preached evolution in the pit to our twelve disciples. Not that Daphne resembles Jesus in any form; those gumboots and raingear are a dead giveaway. Sandals and togas don't come out of her wardrobe for at least ten months of the year. Besides, Salt Spring Island couldn't be farther away from Gethsemane if you tried. That old desert town beside the Dead Sea is a long way from our little bioextravaganza-by-the-Salish-Sea. The mollusks are just a warmup for the three-ring circus here—at least as long as desert dogma pushing fossil fuels and dominating the Earth doesn't get the upper hand.

When we arrived at the dump, the site manager greeted us with an earthy smile. Around him gathered the apostles, sporting their ski goggles and chisels at the ready. He was big and bearded, a deity backlit by a sunbeam piercing through the cloud. When he produced a spare pickaxe out of thin air and told the kids he was a rock hound too, we three adults ascended to the Holy Trinity. The youngest apostle, who received the gift from God, had indeed died and gone to heaven. We unleashed our faithful to scale the cliffs of the pit, wielding their deadly weapons to expose fossils from deep within their muddy graves.

Just so the safety inspectors don't get the impression that islanders are irresponsible about kids with sharp tools in unsanitary conditions, the place referred to as the garbage dump is actually the Transfer Station, where old stuff

143

is transferred from one owner to the next. Recycling was part of our religious indoctrination. We unoffficially call it the Blackburn Mall, an outdoor free store full of outmoded barbeques, big flush toilets, single-pane windows, old blenders, eight tracks, twister games and other detritus of the 20th century. They all look pretty fossil-like amongst the ammonites but are equally prized at the Blackburn Mall. Chipped bathroom tiles come in but go out as mosaic materials. A urinal comes in but goes out as a garden planter. What can't be recycled is eventually transferred to a bigger island at great cost, and handwringing by the volunteer solid waste committee. We headed with the disciples to the pit where those transformations were carried out.

On our walk there, we delivered our first sermon on the evolution of life in the Salish Sea—plate tectonics. To demonstrate this process of continent building, we stopped off at the Blackburn Mall to find a few old floral pattern plates. "Here on the edge of the North American Plate," I raised the two plates like Moses and his stone tablets, "the Pacific Plate slides underneath the North American plate, at the rate our hair grows." I put small heaps of mud on the Pacific Plate to mimic islands. "The Pacific Plate carries groups of islands until they crash into the edge of the North American Plate." The advancing North American plate scrapes the mud islands on to it. "We are inhabitants of a chain of volcanoes from the South Pacific carried over the ocean by this thermal-driven conveyor belt like luggage at the airport. We walk upon the remnants of giant clam-filled coral reefs, blue lagoons full of ammonites and steamy swamps that formed around the atoll as it travelled. The ammonites were swimming around the island when the islands crashed into North America sometime before seventy million years ago." One little hand shoots up, "Is that why we have earthquakes?" The apostles come alive at the mention of earthquakes. "Yes, the area where the plates collide and shake the ground is called the subduction zone."

Eleven-year-olds are typically more interested in the mayhem their pickaxes can wield than in subduction zones, as these sound a little like seduction zones. That will all change one day. I left them with this one last fact: "The shale seam is from an ancient mudslide, maybe triggered by an earthquake, that buried all these creatures. Anything with shells, bones, teeth or scales had the highest likelihood of becoming a fossil. If you remove your protective eye goggles or climb on too steep a slope, your teeth and bones will end up fossilized in a slump of mud as well."

The threat had absolutely no effect. They swarmed the shale beds, scaled the steepest pitches, hung from crumbling cliffs, bashed rocks and each other with abandon and tumbled into the green lagoon at the bottom of the pit teeming with its own primordial algae. The Holy Trinity advanced and delivered the second sermon from the pit—you won't find anything unless you slow down and look closely. After a few minutes of subdued searching, the acolytes found the first ammonite from the late Cretaceous. Its delicate pattern caught the precocious eye of an early adopter. Her small grubby palm revealed the evidence of an ancient extinct cephalopod resembling the shell of its contemporary mollusk cousins, the gastropods: the moon snails of summer tides; and the faithful snails of the bigleaf maple litter. Suddenly their search engines adapted, and all twelve became focussed in a way that only a seventy-million-year-old fossil could focus the young mind.

Each one of the dirty dozen eventually found ammonites, stashing them in their pockets, until the youngest, eyes closest to the earth, started the next Klondike by discovering the first clam. A tiny, perfectly petrified clam came encased in a rock, so like its modern ancestor as to convince its finder that neither time nor evolution has passed between the mudslide and last week's class in the estuary. We had dug for clams earlier with digging sticks like humans have done for millennia: horse clams, butter clams, littleneck clams. The kids had counted the annual growth rings of calcium carbonate shell filtered from the sea. A small finger points out the layers: "One two three, four, five, six. The clam was younger than me before it died." He cradles it even closer when Daphne tells him that the armour encasing its delicate body protected his species from the last mass extinction 66 million years ago when a meteorite sent a fireball round the Earth, incinerating every surface-dwelling creature—a reassuring sign that some life around the Salish Sea will survive the next apocalypse. He pockets it, a birthday present for his mother.

The hunt resumes with the hopes that they find an elasamosaur, a marine reptile that wasn't as lucky as the mollusks. One had been found in 1991 across the Salish Sea on the western shore near the Puntledge River, twelve metres long, half of that neck. Elasamosaurs as a species boiled to death with the rest of the big dinosaurs. The closest ancestors of the ones that survived—ravens, crows and eagles—flapped around above us looking for food transfers. The reptilian ancestors, the painted turtles, hibernate in the mud in the lake down the road, and the small alligator lizards and various snakes doze under the shale, occasionally soaking up enough weak winter sun to raise their heads and eat a sow bug. No giant elasamosaur bones presented themselves, just plenty of "dinosaur eggs." These are concretions that mimic egg or bone-like forms, precipitations of minerals within the layers of mud. We talk about fossils and pseudo-fossils. It is a good metaphor for explaining our current state of political affairs.

To our small crew, the pond at the bottom of the pit resembles the lagoons in which the elasomosaurs swam. It is filled with thick, fluorescent-green algae—greener than the Pacific treefrogs already starting to appear on the early budding salal leaves. We deliver the third and final sermon on the emergence of all life (and death) out of damp places; the appearance of single-celled organisms four billion years ago evolving into life forms as diverse as bacteria causing pneumonia-if-you-fall-in, slime moulds that inhabit some positions of power, fungi and human beings. The sermon covers the broad sweep of the evolution of plants from early algae to the noble Douglas-fir soaring above us at the rim of the pit; how plants began harvesting sunshine, absorbing carbon dioxide, releasing oxygen, storing the carbon in their trunks and roots, changing the atmosphere for mammals like us to survive; then how plate tectonics and processes like mudslides compressed the carbon into coals and other fossil fuels. Humans, mining the accumulated sunshine and burning it through the tail of a pipe, could convert the earth to an atmosphere suited only to those bright green algae, starting the cycle all over again.

Pneumonia is an abstract risk and not half so scary as the threat of extinction of life through climate change—it is the last supper as far as these young apostles are concerned. They are aware, they are anxious, and they want to do the right thing. "Will we go extinct like the elasomosaurs?" They have already written a letter to the prime minister, planted trees, studied eelgrass, signed petitions against pipelines, marched to save the southern resident killer whales, gone plastic-free and presented their ideas at town halls. "The trees stand up for us," said one young acolyte, "we must stand up for them." They struggle like any disciples trying to proselytise a new worldview with only eleven annual growth rings. The Holy Trinity continue to offer libations of hope, a bit of recycling of souls and a few miracles like turning thin air into pickaxes.

Wet, weary, happy and hungry, they eventually crawl out of the pit to retrieve their snacks, replacing them with ammonites, dinosaur eggs and clams. God reclaims his pickaxe and receives his gift of a fossil for being the best host. The transformations continue on around them; a shag rug comes in and goes out as a pond liner. We form a sharing circle, and each one tells the group what they are grateful for in one word, or more: Ammonites, clams, elasamosaurs, pickaxe, each other, alligator lizard, moon snails, playing, mum, Wrangellia, volcanoes, Pacific Plate, snack, ravens, Douglas-fir and the Salish Sea.

MICHAEL REDICAN

QUADRA ISLAND, SAVARY ISLAND

HERON TREES

The wildlife woman wraps each spattered trunk
with flagging tape to show that these
are heron trees

She knows them by the perching nests
and shit and shells all shattered at the base and what we
the neighbors say

we who watched the great birds build
and brood and fly like slaves to feed their chicks
insatiable chatter

till one by one the eagle
took them for a feast while helpless parents screamed
their pterodactyl grief

and now she marks locations on a map
and now explains these trees have full protection
from loggers and the like

and drives off thinking the job well done
while high above the eagle rides the wind
and thinks the same

SAVARY ISLAND

come winter the residents number
close to none
while wind and waves
work away at the bluffs

it's not much more than trees
sand
a glacial remnant
ocean wants back

each spring a little more is gone
a favourite arbutus
six sections of a fence
thirteen steps leading down to the sea

MURRAY REISS

SALT SPRING ISLAND

ISLAND BIOGEOGRAPHY

I could have been a tenrec.
                    In another lifetime.
                                        On another island.
Our evolutionary strategies
                    continents apart
                                        yet the same.

Because while,
                    in the course of evolution,
most mammal groups sensibly discarded
                                        disadvantageous traits,
tenrecs—resemblant of moles, hedgehogs, porcupines, otters—
stubbornly kept theirs.

Bad eyesight? Check.

Fluctuating body temperature? Oh yes.

A cloaca, like that of birds, rather than two separate openings for reproductive
and digestive tracts, like all other mammals? You got it.

Does the male possess a scrotum?
Oh no. He retains his testes inside his abdomen.

Does the female give birth to helpless young, their eyes and ears both closed?
She does.

Does their slow development prolong their vulnerability to predators? You bet.

Every one of these features,

in life's endless struggle against competitor
species and predators,
should disqualify tenrecs at the starting gate.

Baffled zoologists scratch their heads
write reams of peer-reviewed papers pondering
how tenrecs have survived at all
before finally stumbling on the answer—

by getting themselves to an island.

As have I.

Whether Madagascar or Salt Spring, where
        as opposed to the mainland,
competition and predation hold no sway

and islanders
        flaunting our eccentric maladaptations
continue to flourish and (d)evolve.

LINDA ROGERS

SAVARY, CORTES, PENELAKUT, GALIANO AND SALT SPRING ISLAND

THREE SWAN SONGS FROM
THE SALISH SEA

We took turns wearing our copper swan tiara with pearls *en pendant* and saying her name, Tahlequah, or goddess alternates, Tallelayuk, Ceto, Medusa, anything but F-35. She was a mother island, pushing her dead calf to safer waters. We showed her respect and prayed for her and the health of her species. Her ancestors, poets of the sea, swam away from the first continent, and now it was our turn to sing for her and her ocean home.

One summer, with little to do other than read and make sure my younger brothers didn't drown in the waves that washed the white beaches of Savary Island, I read the poet John Donne. "No man is an island," he had written in his *Devotions*. "Truth," my twelve-year-old self realised, "but not ours."

I saw woman islands, basket-makers from Tla'amin, paddle past, imagined swans as graceful as ballerinas and remembered the proverb, "They thought they were burying us, but we were seeds," the fallow secret of Indigenous renaissance. I watched my sisters bust out of the plastic collars choking our fellow beings and rise from the Salish Sea.

My story starts with those Tla'amin women, whose pearls of knowledge were buried in breast-shaped middens. Every Indigenous woman, I learned, was her own Pangea, a volcano of creativity, fire and earth surrounded by water, sustained in her woman functions by cultural teaching, *snuwuyulh.*

At its roots, I was learning, all art is practical, for shelter, cooking, storage, transport and worship. For years, I held the secret ambition to make a woman basket of my own, where I would store my amulets: songs and the swan tiara made by a Kwakwaka'wakw chief.

Before the Whitecomer sailors' vainglorious self-namings, the islands of the Pacific Northwest had names that described their function in the Goddess kitchen. Salt Spring was *Klaathen,* "salt," Kuper was *Penelakut,* which means "log buried on the beach," spoons to stir the sea. How can *Salish*, a word that sounds like water and means "Gift of God(dess)" compare to the name of an imperial Spanish sailor?

My Indigenous friends introduce themselves by saying where they are from. Many Settlers don't know. Some are the descendants of criminals and black sheep who left no trail. Some are slaves who came without baggage, their provenance obliterated by the buying and selling of souls.

Aboriginal kids, stolen by the Oblate Fathers and Sisters of Saint Anne, experienced another kind of slavery in the prison of residential schools, one of the most notorious at Kuper Island (now called Penelakut), across from our sheep farm on the Chemainus River, between the Number Eleven and Tussie Road reserves.

Number Eleven signifies nothing more than the numbers branded on slaves, and when my spirit child, an orphan in the care of older siblings, died by his own hand, I wrote a book called *Say My Name* because everything/everyone has the right to a name and a place of origin, just like the poppies, fritillaries, camas, wild asparagus and berries that breathe the ocean air and ride it to spread their seeds.

Place names are our roots, the matrix I set out to find with my spirit mothers sailing in and out of the clam gardens in the Gulf Islands.

The Indian Act gutted the First Nations, a society that had always held the life functions of women in equal status to that of men, when Settlers decided to impose a colonial model that defined women's roles as craft rather than art. But we persist like the Orca mother pushing her dead calf through turbulent waves, ghost Chinook and floating plastic, enduring love.

The proper renaming of our coastal waters is the first stitch in the reclamation of dignity for Indigenous women, who remain on guard. The Salish Sea, under fresh assault from what the oligarchs call "black gold," and its vulnerable species and salmon culture on the precipice of extinction, is ours to protect. We hiss and bite.

All those years ago, I drew maps in the wet sand at the tide line that would lead me to the mothers who would inspire me to share their sacred knowledge in a protest I would call poems.

Maggie Jack, the fastest blackberry picker in the Pacific Northwest, was born in Squirrel Cove on Cortes Island and spent her later life in a cabin on Tussie Road on Vancouver Island. Like all my spirit mothers, Maggie was mentor to many, and we became best friends after she invited me to join her class in cedar root basket-making.

Maggie was in her sixties, more than twice my age, and had a younger husband she ruled with a stick. Their cedar cabin, missing most of its window glass, was home to the restless spirits of boys damaged by contact.

She looked after the lost boys known as Sam and Them. She had three sons, all of whom travelled to the Other Side camp in tragic circumstances: one in a car accident, another in a fire and finally Sam, her last, in the hideous Sunday afternoon that may have been a pivotal moment in the Penelakut Island people taking back their name and was an epiphanous moment in my life.

Maggie, Vernon and I had spent many happy hours asking the trees to lend us bark for balers and roots for baskets. The best roots were the ones that grew straight through the sandy soil on the banks of the Chemainus River, to fresh water. They were purposeful roots, and we thanked them for their thirst.

There was a lot of humour about my backward way of doing things. I am left-handed, *a la sinestra*, and that is a tolerated anomaly in Maggie's culture, which embraces all kinds of difference and defines gender as a fluid entity.

When Maggie was diagnosed with a recurrence of stomach cancer, she asked me to find the healer who made medicine from yew bark. Sadly, he was at his winter camp, somewhere in the United States, and I did not find him in time. I later learned that yew sap is the basis for *tamoxifen*, now a common drug used for preventing and treating breast cancer.

On Mother's Day, I went by the rez to pick up Sam and Them to visit Maggie in the hospital. Her terrified "boys" refused to go with me. Sam asked for money. I refused because they intended to call the bootlegger.

On the way home from visiting Maggie, I bought groceries for Sam and Them, but when I got there, the cabin was empty except for a bird in the house, one crow hovering on her windowsill.

A curtain flapped in the wind, interrupting the deepest silence.

The next morning, I heard from Cowichan elder Leonard Peter that the boys had gone to Penelakut Island to borrow spirit duplicator (I type this phrase in astonishment) from the residential school, their chamber of horrors in the innermost circle of hell. Sam and Them should not have taken their wounded souls anywhere near there.

They all died drinking the school poison that night. Maggie kept on waiting for them, a horrible death protracted by her priest and her doctor, who forbade revealing what had happened to her boys and delayed her journey to the Other Side.

When she passed, I gathered cedar root baskets from friends and filled them with wildflowers for her funeral service, while, outside the church, band members collected money and argued with relatives from Squirrel Cove, who were there to take her home for burial. I remember Brother Amos singing "Amazing Grace," the wildflowers in Maggie's baskets, the wailing of friends and relatives and the sound of gravel when the Squirrel Cove contingent made a fast getaway with her coffin.

Forty years later, Maggie is mostly smells in blessed memory: the perfumes of lupin and dog roses, the intoxicating summer scents of cedar and blackberries, salmonberries, her pungent beaver stew, her smoked fish. What she taught me was respect for the mother tasks: feeding our young indigenous food and telling them stories so that they could find their way through the forest to the life-giving waters, their own sound walks.

I learned from Maggie, who was wise in ways that the accomplished book-learners I knew as a child could not touch, that I could learn more from life itself. Books were only little moons reflecting the light available all around us.

Maggie, my island mother, taught me to drown my books and to watch and listen. Now when I hear the activist singing of her young relative, water protector Ta'Kaiya Blaney, I hear my friend. Maggie's last gift to me is the understanding that "death shall have no dominion," when you are a teacher.

Shortly after Maggie died, I followed the wake of an elderly cousin, "Canada's Grandma Moses," as she performed her own miracle, changing skins in the wilderness as we had when we were wild things living in fern and cedar branch forts.

Elisabeth Hopkins, cousin of the tormented poet Gerard Manley Hopkins and the explorer Peter Skene Ogden, followed the explorer's path to Galiano Island.

159

Galiano inspired her last and most beautiful transformation. Blending the mythology of her childhood on the island of Jersey and the spirit of her adopted home, she painted flora and anthropomorphic fauna with Pelican watercolours.

Elisabeth gave up intense gardening for equally passionate representation of her Settler world, where all my relations enjoyed her never-ending birthday parties, her equivalent of the ceremonial life she observed in Indigenous communities.

We met her on the Gulf Island ferry, of course. Because she had been searching for us, she knew us right away. Hopy aka Dizzy Lizzie mentored my children, passing on her view of the world: all ducks have swan potential.

When she died, my sons, her infant pallbearers, dropped their gentle cousin, dressed in a bridal nightgown for her holy groom, under the tree outside the Anglican church in Ganges and unwrapped three Zero bars, their shared sacrament.

Hopy taught me that women can change shape and shift in new directions, moving gently to the light. She also taught me ageism is just a word. Just as volcanoes emerge from the ocean, we rise again and again, as did the slave descendants who arrived on our shores Post-Emancipation, looking for their island in the sun.

The third swan in my holy trinity was Mairuth Sarsfield, who became my friend and spirit guide when I worked on her last unpublished manuscript, a book about the African-American settlement of Salt Spring Island. Born in Montreal, the activist, documentarian, diplomat and author of *No Crystal Stair,* a memoir whose title came from Langston Hughes, knew that celestial navigation was a risky business.

She had loved and lost in a lifetime of dignity and grace.

Curiosity about the Afro-American diaspora brought Mairuth to the salt island, a grotesque irony because her final task was more salt in her wounds. Mairuth, who lost both her children in terrible twists of fate—her son in a car accident soon after graduation from law school, and her daughter, also a filmmaker, to early-onset breast cancer—did not see the publication of her last book, the struggle of freed slaves to put down roots in their island home.

The stars were fickle, but Mairuth, the *griot,* never lost her way even though she had no idea where her ancestors had come from. Her mission was to witness and record the tides of racism. She died when the tide was out, a black swan exhausted on the beach.

My sister Mairuth taught me to persist. There will always be storms and loss at sea, but good mothers teach us to carry on with their swan songs.

We endure. When spirit mothers, exhausted by *skookumchuck,* worn like sea glass, lie down on the beaches of the Salish Sea to be found by others, sometimes little girls who admire their colour and shape and continue the fight to protect what we love, mothers and daughters, all my relations, sharing the swan tiara.

> *Those are pearls that were (her) eyes;*
> *Nothing of (her) that doth fade,*
> *But doth suffer a sea-change*
> *Into something rich and strange.*

–William Shakespeare, from "The Tempest"

CHRISTINE SMART

THE SALISH SEA

SAGA

In Saanich Inlet, we sailed a sloop
a generation ago, the water swarmed
with salmon and herring, a pod of orcas.

Down the ladder submerged in the warming ocean,
the slither of jellies on skin, a diaphanous
bloom scatters as I swirl in its midst.

Near Senanus Island, in a small cove
nestled between Tsartlip and Tsawout, I swam

with you in my belly, the chill
shocked you into flip turns: you learned to swim
inside, warm within cold, me floating on my back

buoyant, weightless. A dozen people paddled a dugout,
a drum beating the rhythm of their oars: training
ground for young warriors, faces painted, voices ringing across the water.

On the sailboat, we drift between islands,
tides and currents hold memory,
ebb and flow. The present

encapsulates the past,
stories of former lives and loves: a blowdown
in a gale, mainsail in the water.

How we ran the boat up on a reef,
smell of seaweed and fear, on a falling tide,
me primed to give birth.

What we choose to remember and forget.

The boat, a passage, reliant on wind,
the sails luff, in irons, holding us
steady in this glassy moment.

STEVEN ROSS SMITH

GALIANO ISLAND

BUOYED

I am *is*
am sailing on the saline
Salish, the lush, delicious Salish Sea
    not sailing... paddling actually, dip & pull
splashed seadrops shushing
slipping away astern

I am *is*
sashaying... shouldering actually
    tack & skim, stroking on steely wetskin
beside bellycurved pocked rocks
seabubbled bevelled belled
gliding beside bobbing rustish arbutus skins, flaked
curled vessels dashed & dotting the ripples
peppering my briny syntax that speaks my sea
the salty Salish

I am *is*
tottering in Salish wave-wash, beside
a pair of humped-running
sleek-swimming shoreline-scrambling otters
    I'm not too-tottery to be awed by their clever company
    & honoured to glide beside
    their wet-furred nimble rambling

I am *is*
paler than this sea, pinkening in sun's blaze
    unlike the oystercatcher, black-suited, Halloween-garbed
    neon-orange-billing the Salish shore
    snoutdipping for limpet tidbits, beaking my attention

I am   *is*
tillerman torquing, feathering my blade
  not paddling exactly... but guiding
  not guiding exactly... but yielding... not yielding fully
  but praising... praying actually... not praying exactly
  but reverent... not reverent exactly
  but mystified... not that exactly
  but humming as I beach beside tinkly shell & pebble music
  humming my humbled throaty *ommmm*

I am *one*
with the Salish Sea
  its kiss, its salt upon my lips
not *one* exactly...
I am   *is*
upon it

once *was*
from it

GEORGE SZANTO

GABRIOLA ISLAND

HOME TO HOME

The sand and gravel driveway to our home on Gabriola Island crosses a wetlands that we call the Bog. It is alive with frogs and birds, larvae and skaters. A few weeks ago, I noted, across the driveway, a newly wet trail leading from the western section of the Bog to the eastern. Evidence that something had crawled out of the water on one side, back in on the other?

The largest part of the Bog lies to the west, part on our land and part belonging to a neighbor, Dave. To the east, most of the Bog belongs to another neighbor, Sharon. Years back when Sharon's partner was still alive, he asked a friend with a backhoe to deepen a section of his part of the Bog, thereby creating a pool free of spirea, locally called hardhack because it is indeed hard to hack. The hardhack is rooted in the water, growing up to two meters into the air. To remove it, the backhoe is essential.

I checked both ends of the moist trail and found a point of departure from one section of the Bog's hardhack and a point of re-entry to the other. The animal had engineered a scrambled pathway between shrubs and roots to make for easier climbing up the bank from the water. On the other side, it had flattened the grasses and small weeds to create a chute back down into the Bog. What kind of animal it was I had no idea. But clearly with engineering training of its own. In the past there have been sightings of the occasional mink on the land around us. I talked with Sharon about the mysterious pilgrim. Yes, she said, I've seen it swimming in the pond. It's a beaver.

And a large beaver—she estimates its weight at fifty to sixty pounds. Likely a female. Sharon has seen her basking in mud on the side of the pond next to the house.

I'm told that years ago beavers were not uncommon in the Bog, mainly at its westernmost end. Most beavers in the wild, where there are animal predators as well as human trappers who deem beavers to be nuisance animals, live ten years or less. But on a protected piece of land like an island, like Gabriola, they've been known to live twenty-five to thirty years. Sharon wonders whether this is an offspring of that beaver family, come back here to the Bog to die. Another explanation: because she's so big, possibly she's pregnant and has returned to give birth. At age thirty? Dubious. But whatever her private reason for taking up residence in the Bog, she's found at least a temporary home here.

For my wife, Kit, and me, the island is our permanent home. Several years ago, I wrote a book about this home of ours, called *Bog Tender,* a year of life beside our wetlands.

These days I'm a bit obsessed with the notion of *home*. Kit and I are in our late seventies, and we are building a new abode here. Not by the Bog but, yes, on Gabriola. This is the island we've discovered we belong to. Some say we must be slightly mad to make a house-building commitment at our age. But we see it as a hedge against assisted living—that is, the chance to live in a more sensible section of the island because we want to stay here. Our present home is on the highest point of Gabriola. We look from our living room and kitchen, from our two upstairs bedrooms, seventy kilometers down the Pylades and Trincomali Channels across to the Malahat. A magnificent view, but in the winter of 2016, we had masses of snow, resplendent, but it kept us from driving down the road to our home for nearly three weeks, and for four days, even with front-wheel drive and snow tires, we were unable to get us up our road to the drive. The car slipped into a snowbank: I called BCAA, Can you pull us out? Is your road cleared? No. Sorry, we can't send our tow out onto an icy road.

Twenty-eight years ago when we bought this property, five acres of uncleared land and the Bog, we also bought a half-acre lot close to the village center. Where, as I write, we are building this new home. That is to say, our contractor Stuart and his crew are doing the work, Stuart being the man who also built our present house with its grand view; years before that, he had built what has been for nearly two and a half decades our guest cottage, my studio, where we had lived several half years while still spending part of our time in Montreal. So Stuart will have built three homes for us on Gabriola. Because he does fine work, that's why. To compound our pleasure in working with those we thoroughly trust, the architect who designed our present house is also the person who gave shape to our forthcoming home on the smaller lot. Loyalty to the highest quality is easy on a small island.

The lot the new house stands on is dry, even deep down where the water table should lie. Where we are still living, the below-surface land is a lot wetter, although few would believe this after spending the summer of 2018 here, no rain for ten weeks. The only thing that kept flowering plants and vegetables alive was our deep well. We draw water from 362 feet below the surface, luckily with superior pressure—over sixteen gallons a minute. When the hole for the foundation of this house was hacked, through sandstone, the excavator found flowing water near the surface, which ran dry in March before the foundation was laid down. In October, when serious rains began again, the floor of the crawlspace cracked and flooded the area—happily built on a lower and higher level. The water found its depth, pooling in only the deeper part. What to be done? I wondered about stocking it with trout: fresh fish year-round. Stuart suggested we deal with the flooding the way a commercial fisherman would deal with his boat filling with water—cut a hole down in the keel so the water can flow out again. Which is what we decided. With a jackhammer, Stuart hacked a hole so all the water could gather in the same place, and dropped a sump pump down with a switch that turns the thing on when an inch of water gathers there. Perfectly dry crawlspace for eighteen years.

Not so for the new small lot. There's no water down there. In the past, neighbours have drilled. Many dry wells. We figured we wouldn't even try. Several people on the island have dug large cisterns and built their houses over captured rainwater. There's no lack of water on the island in winter, spring too, just an absence of large retention basins. Retention of water is a fine solution for seasonal water flow. We wanted a similar system. Stuart took our request to the regional district. No, sorry, no longer allowed. Why not? New regulations put in place a very few years back: since there's no sewage collection on the island, every house needs a septic system. The septic field must be thirty-five metres from the house, and far enough from the cistern to avoid any chance of contamination. So we will have to construct above-ground cisterns.

One of the few advantages of relative lack of water on the smaller lot is slow tree growth. Since we needed to clear that part of the lot where the house would stand, a good many second-growth firs on the property had to come down. When we saw the narrow rings on the logs (a highly valued quality for cabinet makers and builders), we allowed ourselves to be convinced that the wood should stay on the property, transformed to flooring and kitchen cabinets. This will happen. The boards now lie, covered, drying, up at our present house. Soon they will get a final milling, be kiln-dried and ready for use: wood reincarnated.

We've lived in several parts of the world—France, Mexico, California, Wyoming, Boston, Montreal. We have enjoyed living in all our houses, but none of those locations have given us a full sense of belonging in or to those spaces. In the process of buying the land on which our present home stands, I came here to look at the property. It's a long and narrow lot, around seventy meters wide and a third of a kilometer long, cut in half by the Bog. The realtor's description stated: *an engineer's challenge.* Twenty-six years ago, on a warm September afternoon, I sat beside the Bog in silence for over an hour. Juncos, towhees, sparrows of varieties I would have to learn the names of and a small garter snake made their appearances. Suddenly, a pair of pileated woodpeckers landed on a branch over my head and watched me. I imagined them muttering, Okay, you're welcome here. I felt very much at home. We bought the engineer's challenge. After twenty-six years, we've come to feel that this has been our home forever, long awaiting our arrival. Maybe twenty-six years from now, we'll feel the same about our forthcoming home. It'll still be on Gabriola.

For the past couple of weeks, the beaver's water-departure point and its chute back down into the Bog have been covered with leaves. I've seen no evidence that it has crossed to our side of the wetlands. It seems her pilgrimage has stopped, and she is now a permanent resident in our neighbour's pond. Maybe her engineering days are behind her. She's found her new home. Good for her.

NANCY J. TURNER

PROTECTION ISLAND

ROWING AROUND THE ISLAND

R owboats have always been my favourite way of travelling on water. There is something special about the rhythm and regular surge that propels you forward. Rowing is the nautical equivalent to "Slow Food." When I was a kid, I spent many happy hours with my sister and our friend Joan, sporting our bulky life jackets, rowing in a bulky clinker-built rowboat along the shores of Lake Cowichan.

Over the years, what with going to university, raising children, teaching and the entire maelstrom of activities that capture our lives, I was swept away in other directions, deprived of rowboats and their pleasures. For a brief period, we owned a beautiful but aged carvel-built rowboat named *Tsuki,* the Japanese name for "Moon." *Tsuki* was built by a Japanese Canadian boatwright interned in the Interior during World War II. He built the boat in Nelson, in southeastern British Columbia, and it had been used on Kootenay Lake ever since. Ownership had fallen to one of our friends, and unable to look after her, he gave her to us. We bought a boat trailer and brought *Tsuki* back to Victoria, intending to patch up her cracks (which had been sealed with black tar) and launch her on the coast. But she had been neglected too long, and the shaped planks had started to rot at the bow. In the end, we returned her to her birthplace in the Kootenays, to live out her days at the Nelson Museum.

Decades and decades later, my husband, Bob, and I bought our place on Protection Island, off Nanaimo, and almost immediately our daughters ordered a small rowboat for me. This boat, which we called *Nancy's Calypso,* is in a class called Lady Slipper, designed and built by master boatbuilder John Rabenek of Nanaimo. *Calypso* sits on a small boat trailer that we can easily pull behind our electric golf cart down to a boat launch at the south end of the island. When I climb in and push off, I enter my own world. It's hard to describe; it's challenging, exhilarating, comforting and relaxing, all at the same time.

Invariably I spot harbour seals lounging on the log booms I row past on the west side of Protection Island. They slip easily into the water and follow my boat, poking their sleek heads out so I can admire and greet them, then sinking effortlessly and soundlessly beneath the waves, only to appear in some other location a short time later. Other creatures frequent the log booms and shoreline. I often see families of river otters galumphing along the logs, or raccoons scavenging along the beach. Great blue herons stand like statues, staring down into the water, patiently waiting for an unsuspecting fish to dart by. In early spring, when the herring congregate in large schools to spawn along the shoreline, huge flocks of gulls gather on the log booms, and swirl around overhead. Cormorants also perch on the booms at times, hanging their wings out to dry. Eagles, and sometimes turkey vultures, ride the air currents overhead, and kingfishers, with their sharp rattling calls, speed along the shore, stopping to hover at times then plunge into the water for the catch. We also have a flock of purple martins that arrive in the late spring and fill the summer air with their distinctive twittering from high up in the blue sky.

From the vantage point of my rowboat, I observe the world and all its activities. My island neighbours often motor by in their small boats, always with a cheerful greeting. Sometimes the harbour patrol boat passes by, leaving a wake that gently rocks my boat. Always sailboats and yachts motor in and out of the harbour, and I imagine where they are heading—maybe to Alaska, maybe to Hawaii. Of course, there are always kayakers, other rowers and dragon boat crews working their paddles in sync, with the drummer calling out the beat. I have to be careful that I don't bump into anyone, since I am facing backwards. Occasionally I bump into a small log, but my relatively slow speed averts any damage. It's soothing; I easily find my own rhythm for the oars and fall into a meditative state of just being.

As I make my way around the island, I see special landmarks. There is the Dinghy Dock Pub, famous for its ambiance and camaraderie; people come from all over the world, taking the foot ferry over from Nanaimo to experience this floating pub. I know it is a place of great value because once I saw a rainbow whose end hovered exactly overtop of the Dinghy Dock. The little ferry, formerly a lifeboat from the big BC Ferries, takes island residents and Dinghy Dock customers back and forth every hour. I often see it coming and going as I row by. My little boat slips easily under the gangway connecting the dock with the island. Then come all the anchored boats dispersed around the west end of the channel between Protection and Newcastle Islands. Some people live on their boats, and we get to know each other over time. More greetings, conversations about the weather, the seabirds and the events and issues of the day.

I greet my favourite boats as old friends: *Nanamuk*, *Kokomo*, *Seabreeze* and others. I notice if they are missing from their anchorages, and wonder where they have gone and how long they will be away. I look across to Newcastle and think about the history of this place. It doesn't take much imagination to put myself back in the days before the Europeans arrived here, to picture Snuneymuxw families spread all along the channel, pulling their cedar dugout canoes onto the beaches, camping under framework shelters covered with dense mats of cattail and tule, harvesting their food, preparing their fishnets and duck nets of stinging nettle fibre, and teaching their children the right way to do things: Always be respectful of other life, always be thankful for the gifts they provide, always share and never waste. They would be speaking in their own Hul'q'umi'num language, which embodies terms for all of these things, as well as names for every cove, creek and point of land.

In the spring, they would be digging clams, harvesting mussels and sea urchins, and pulling up masses of herring spawn-covered eelgrass. In summer, they would be picking berries—red huckleberries, trailing blackberries, salal berries, thimbleberries—and harvesting camas bulbs along the coastal bluffs, cooking them in underground pits until they were as sweet as chestnuts. In fall, they would pick the little tart crab apples and hunt swans, geese, ducks, seals, deer and other game. They used the islands as a base for fishing for salmon as well: springs in the early part of the year, sockeye and pinks in the summer and coho and chum, or dog salmon, in the fall. I know of rock carvings made by the Old Ones in some locations on the Protection Island shoreline, powerful and beautiful images that symbolize interactions with the spirit world, although I have never seen them myself.

Rowing east through the channel between the islands at mid-tide, I am treated to an amazing conglomeration of sea life—sand dollars, streams of emerald-green eelgrass, sea wrack and other marine algae, crater-like holes where butter clams, littlenecks and cockles are buried deep in the muddy sand, and masses of the more recently arrived Japanese oysters and Manila clams with their violet inner shells.

After the discovery of coal in and around these islands, the lives of the

Snuneymuxw changed forever, as miners and settlers swarmed into their territory. Some people became wealthy, but the land suffered and so did many Snuneymuxw. Trees were cut down to make props for the coalmine tunnels and lumber for buildings. By the time the last coal mine in Nanaimo closed, the landscape had changed forever, although the forests have regenerated to some extent. Newcastle Island is now a protected marine park run by the Snuneymuxw people, and called *Saysutshun*, meaning "training for running"—one of the original activities that took place there long ago.

As I row alongside Saysutshun, I look for the profiles of my favourite big Douglas-fir trees on the island, and greet their familiar silhouettes. I see my favourite big cottonwoods along the shore, and giant bigleaf maples spread their mossy branches, providing shade for the visitors. Halfway along the channel is a small rocky peninsula projecting from Protection Island. It has a marker to warn boaters of the hazardous shallows. On occasion I have had to hop out and pull my boat through these narrows in the lowest tides. Frequently I see a covey of black oystercatchers, with their bright orange beaks and feet and their plaintiff calls, and a pair of red-tailed hawks circling. As well, the ever-present and charismatic ravens charm me with their raucous calls, which I like to imitate.

Once into deeper water, I can look down to see the bottom alive with crabs of all sizes, scurrying about in some kind of mass choreographed underwater dance. I start to feel the swells of the outer channel surging into the gap, and I have to work hard to progress through the big waves, but my little boat bobs over them without a single drop of water coming in. As soon as I have passed the big swells and get out into the main channel, I easily ride the waves, getting propelled along with every wave twice as far as I could by rowing alone. This is the exhilarating part: rowboat surfing. I pass the houses of friends, including the house of our buddies Doug and Melissa. Melissa loves paddling her kayak as much as I love rowing, and whenever we can, we row and paddle together.

Seals keep following me, and every once in a while, I glimpse a shiny head popping up behind me, just to see what I'm about. In the fall and winter, we also have huge sea lions in the main channel. I call them the "bad boys." They are the males of the Southern California sea lions and the northern Steller's sea lions, who come together in small groups to pursue the great salmon runs. They seem especially fond of the fall chum salmon, and their loud barking lasts long into the night. Sometimes, when I have to row quite close to them, they shoot almost out of the water nearby the boat, giving me a start. But they have never tried to hurt me or my boat in any way; I can only assume they are as curious about me as I am about them. They have bad breath and loud and boisterous voices, but they add adventure and excitement to my journey.

Along the southern part of the island, I am sometimes overtaken by the Gabriola Island ferry, with its regular runs to and from Nanaimo. Of course, I enjoy the waves created by the ferry, but have to be careful to orient my boat so it doesn't get swamped. Finally rounding the southern point, with the sad name, Gallows Point, I skirt around the small lighthouse, past the cove near where the island coal mine opened, around the public dock and back to the ramp, where Bob is waiting with the boat trailer to help me haul *Calypso* out of the water. By this time, often the sun is just starting to go down, and we are treated with peachy-coloured skies to the west. If I'm lucky, I'll get to do it all again tomorrow.

M.C. WARRIOR

GABRIOLA ISLAND

LOCK BAY BY NIGHT

three in the morning, a hard
October gale blowing through the Strait
and the tourists—the pleasure boaters,
the sporties—are all tucked safely
in some breakwater's lee, clearing
a path for the working water, this coast's
arterial blood—tugs, ferries, freighters,
fish boats and their packers.

sitting on the beach at Lock Bay, in the lee
of Orlebar Point, i watch navigation lights
emerge behind Entrance Island and feel
a tug's diesels throbbing in the stirrups
of my ears as it hauls southeast
towards Vancouver harbour's
permanent false dawn.

a sea lion barks nearby, so close
i can almost inhale its stench
and once more i am twenty-one,
drunk with the sounds, the smells,
the sights and the stories of
a world utterly new to me.

a world where high lead whistles summoned
logs literally the size of small houses up
sidehills that only a goat would tackle unpaid,
where strikes and blacklists, violent
death and crippling injury
were not the stuff of folksong but threads
in the weave of everyday life.

the running lights begin to dim,
the diesels fade. i turn back
along the footpath towards home, to light
a morning fire from wood we felled,
bucked, hauled in a wheelbarrow,
and split ourselves, wood from the five acres
to which we've fled hoping
that some trace of that world of our youth
still lingers here on one of the islands
that gave it birth.

ALISON WATT

MITLENATCH ISLAND

IT SEEMS TO MOVE AWAY AS YOU
APPROACH IT

We talk about our hair. Length, colour, amount of new grey; our weight—Nancy's lost a few pounds this year, I've put on a few; the small signs of aging, marking our bodies like tattoos, wrinkles, looseness, the skin letting go.

This summer on Mitlenatch Nancy is preoccupied with her move to Monterey, her new job—lots of stress, responsibility.

I think of my mother. I look out over the sea, the heat which baked into her bones as a child, summering at nearby Point Holmes—this was the light she knew, this sea—just so, the shade of blue, just these smells, hot, salt shore, these white cumulus clouds trimming the horizon. And life, which once seemed such a long unfolding, which stretched ahead of me with infinite turnings and possibilities—as if composed of multiplying rather than disappearing moments—now seems sparingly passed out. Such a short journey from nut-brown girl running through blue days to old woman, ebbing breath, on a hospital bed. My own children have grown from infants to adolescents so fast it is as if accomplished under some spell of forgetfulness, a slight of time's hand.

I wrote this in my journal the summer after my mother died, and I was spending my annual week on a tiny island in the northern reach of the Salish Sea, with my friend Nancy.

I first set foot on Mitlenatch Island when I was twenty-four. I spent a whole summer there as a B.C. park naturalist the year before the government replaced the position with volunteer wardens.

Nancy also once worked as a park naturalist. She and I have spent one week here as wardens every summer for most of twenty-five years. She lives in California. For a handful of days each year, we have a long uninterrupted conversation with each other, ourselves, and with the island.

Mitlenatch is within the territories of the Coast Salish. Their name for the island means "calm water all around." To the Kwagiulth people, *mah-kwee-*

184

lay-lah meant "it looks close, but seems to move away as you approach it."

Every May almost 4,000 glaucous-winged gulls arrive to nest among the grasses. From then until they leave in September, the air is filled with their cries. When visitors ask us how we stand it, we are surprised to be reminded of the cacophony; for us it is simply the soundtrack of the island, like the wind and waves.

The cold tides that sweep around Vancouver Island from the outer ocean push in from both the north and south. They meet restlessly, stirring up deeper layers, in the waters around Mitlenatch. The rich broth nourishes not just gulls but nesting colonies of cormorants, guillemots and crows, bald eagles, a family of ravens, marauding peregrines and scores of moulting harlequin ducks. River otters beat trails from the sea through the grass. Sea lions linger after the herring spawns of early spring. Hundreds of female harbour seals gather here to bear their pups. Transient killer whales hunt them, gliding swiftly, silently, close to shore. In recent years, humpback whales have returned to the strait.

Sometimes I am startled to remember that the island is inert, basalt dragged here on an ocean plate from near the equator, scattered with granite boulders dropped by receding glaciers of the last ice age. Its meadows are embroidered with wildflowers, camas and chocolate lilies, sea blush and brodiaea, blue-eyed Mary. Its shore is seeded with sea stars, chitons, snails, mussels, clams; the island set like a heart coupled to light, quickened by spring, slowed by winter. Time elaborated migrations, dormancies, flowering, fruiting, birth, predation. And from it all now flows something that can only be felt as charisma.

Nancy and I have woven our own ecology into this island. The complex history of our friendship, the year we backpacked Europe together, bird-watching and reading Russian novels aloud. Beginnings and endings; our first serious relationships; arrivals, departures, relocations of homes and hearts. Tides which brought us together (our living for a time in the same city) and drew us apart (my marriage to her ex-husband) and together again until we can scan the distance from this shore, the point from which the years stretch behind us luxuriantly, and the sparer ones ahead recede as if the more closely we approach them, the farther away they seem. Like the memories of my mother.

At the beach house I ran free and wild the whole summer, my mother wrote in a short memoir. *The days seemed to stretch on in endless sunshine.*

The sea glittered in the hot sun and sent up shimmering heat waves that made the Gulf Islands waver and change shape.

That girl was to grow into a lovely green-eyed woman with delicate wrists and a penchant for feckless men. This summer I worry the strands of her life, searching for its narrative, things I need to understand and remember. Talking it over with Nancy.

We anchor ourselves on this rock for a short time, and we find good holding ground year after year, sharing in the faith that carries the birds back. Which is a kind of optimism, an antidote to the despairs of our times. And what we speak of less often—that we alight on Earth for a brief season.

If we are lucky, we are provided with a good mother, a good friend.

The sweetest lullabies I ever heard were the sounds of waves on the shore and the wind through the branches of the pine trees, my mother wrote.

Sometimes at night, Nancy and I lie in the field, the summer wind shaking the dry seedpods of wildflowers, and watch blizzards of stars blowing through pure darkness. Out beyond the island, we hear the humpbacks breathing.

BOB WEEDEN

SALT SPRING ISLAND

PERFUME FROM STONES

To build something new, first take apart something old.

At Ruckle Point's steep foreshore, you stand on sandstones formed 100 million years ago, give or take a week. The smooth brown-grey ledges, comfortable underfoot, have cracks that flood with water in December rains. Sometimes, in January, dense cold air from B.C.'s Interior rushes down the Fraser Valley and rides the shivering breezes onto Salt Spring Island. Water in the sandstone cracks freezes, and then expands with force, to deepen old fissures and start new ones. Bits of stone flake off.

Winter rains slowly dissolve the chemical bonds gluing crystals together and release salts, oxides and clay minerals. Now the velvet moss grows thick and green, inviting us to caress it. Where the hair-like false roots of moss meet the rock, the exchanges between rock and moss create complex acids that speed the weathering process.

Every rock has a memory of the extreme pressures that stuck it together. These old latent forces are greatest deep in the rock. At the surface, only the weight of the atmosphere counteracts this inside-out force. Anything from the outside that weakens the bonds of surface crystals is helped by a final push from inside. Pop!

Grain by grain, flake by flake, the sandstone ledge crumbles. The pieces accumulate in cracks and hollows. To become soil, they need the remnants of life. As sure as death and gravity, organic crumbs will come. They will be fragments of storm-tossed kelp, feathers from preening ducks, bits of wind-pruned branches, wisps of grass, leaves from the arbutus and Garry oak that grow on uplands just over your shoulder. They will be clams, dropped by famished gulls, which bounce into deep crevices. Oh, yes, otter poop, raccoon scats, forgotten crusts from picnics—let's just call it Gaia's dandruff.

Old rock has combined with old life to make soil. To work our miracle we need only seeds, the commonplace marvel that bridges the generations of flowering plants. Among the flowers that will grow here on the salty hem of our island are the exquisite blue-eyed Mary, pink sea blush, and hardy golden stonecrop. In spring each seed will send a fibrous hand downward and a green shoot skyward. Water and nutrients will flow within them. From that busy elemental traffic will come perfume from stones.

TWO OAKS FALL INTO MEMORY

In the waving blue meadows of the Salish Sea there is an island of trees called Chu'an. In this forest there is an island of grass. In this meadow of small grow two oaks, an island of tall. They grow so close together that, in accommodating each other's elbowing limbs, they outline one tree. They share breeze and bright sun and intimacies in the dark soil. They are friends of hawk and woodpecker, of strollers and scribblers and image-takers, of farmers making hay and young cattle in heifervescent play. They shelter lovers and wedding parties and sleeping children.

Then, at the end of our winter of hard rain and romping winds, their roots pull out of the sodden soil. Slowly they spread apart. Gently they fall. The community collects its memories and finds them beautiful.

Trees do that to people, especially trees so huge they humble us, the ones that live longer than we do, that endure more. While we keep tearing around, they are Sondheim's immoveable ones, glad to harbour other lives while we keep our distance.

Consider, for example, the Golden Spruce that grew along the Yakoum River in Haida Gwaii. Less than three hundred years old when Grant Hadwin cut it down in 1997, the Haida people considered it sacred. *K'iid K'iyaas*, they called it: "the Elder Spruce." Whites who found it much later were amazed, and one timber surveyor said in 1924, "a bit overcome by its strangeness." Botanists were moved to call it Picea sitchensis 'Aurea,' the golden and splendid and beautiful spruce. When a renegade logger, acting alone, felled it, many wanted to keep it alive in memory. Carve a totem, some said. Mill it for guitar wood, said others. Give chunks to local artists, they said. In the end, the tree stayed where it fell, resurrecting itself as a nurse log for seedlings. Conservationists made grafts, and clones are in collections all over the world. Still, there was only one sacred tree, glowingly alive in its forest home, and it is gone.

Or consider The Sentinel, a bald cypress near Orlando, Florida. Germinating from a seed a century before Moses lived, it thrived in the swampy soils, survived thousands of hurricanes and innumerable summer grass fires. Seminole people loved it, guided on its 118-foot top, and showed it to Ponce de Leon when he came in 1524. Then the British idea of land and property grabbed us. A man, who had built a fortune from cypress timber made into rail ties that wouldn't rot, bought the land around the big tree. He logged the forest but left the giant, now renamed The Senator because the rich man went into politics. He gave the tree and eleven acres to the town as a park.

On January 16, 2012, the local fire department raced to the park to find The Senator "fully involved." They couldn't save it. They found a pile of charred twigs in the hollow base of the tree, a traditional place for lonely and meditative and secretive villagers to shelter. A young woman confessed to having been there that night to try one last time to kick a meth addiction. She lit a fire, woke up coughing, climbed back over the fence and scurried home. Convicted, she paid a fine of $14,000, did 250 hours of manual labour and served a suspended sentence of two and one-half years.

The Senator is gone, but its genes linger. Many people over the decades had tried, unsuccessfully, to find viable seeds in its cones. In 1997, a horticulturalist visiting the tree picked up a branch to switch away pesky mosquitoes and later dropped it on his car seat. He took it to a friend, a savvy gardener who loved bald cypress, who made ten bud grafts from the flyswatter. Seven grew. One, now eighteen years old, was planted near the base of the original tree. They call it The Phoenix.

We have both roots and wings. We come by them honestly; they help us survive. But being what we are, we long to fly when we have been stuck too long, and we long to settle—to dwell, fully and passionately—when we tire of being in full flight. I think North Americans have been on the move too much for too long, and yearn to have a home instead of houses. Maybe that's why we hug trees.

We had depended on the sturdy presence of our twinned Salt Spring Island oaks. Then they fell, and suddenly we knew their roots and ours had been joined all our lives. They had become sacred.

In subtle and varied ways, we as individuals and communities create around us a sacred geography. Undistinguished spaces become points of permanent meaning. Time becomes a necklace of events named and remembered, a calendar of our cherished history. A landscape becomes our landscape, where fulfillment and grace are ours in exchange for our love. It becomes the home of our heart, *la querencia*.

REX WEYLER

CORTES ISLAND

BLUE DASHER

The dragonfly's eye appears green, then blue-green, then with a tinge of reddish-yellow and suddenly green again. A gentle summer breeze sways the fir tree canopy high above, but down here all is still. Dragonflies have five eyes. Three small black ancillary eyes and two large compound eyes that dominate the head. Each large eye contains up to thirty-thousand facets, each about one ten-millionth of a square millimeter and facing a unique direction, allowing the insect to see in virtually every direction. The facets refract sunlight like a diamond, changing colour as I slowly tilt my head.

The insect is hyper-sensitive to movement, so if I move too quickly, it may flee. The head is white and the body a powder blue. This is a male blue dasher, *Pachydiplax longipennis*, meaning (not what one first suspects) "long wings," so-named by naturalist Karl Herman Burmeister in Argentina in 1839. An image of a blue dragonfly appears on a four-thousand-year-old Egyptian amulet. Dragonflies can be seen depicted on Hopi pottery, Japanese woodcuts, Art Nouveau jewelry, in a Basho haiku and in my wife's wild paintings.

This particular blue dasher sits on a tiny rock islet in a rain pool, one wing reflected in the murky water. The pool fills a depression in gray biotite granite, the bedrock of this region, which forms a small island in a lake. Locally, we call this isle of granite, covered with fir, hemlock, cedar and arbutus trees, "Turtle Island." It sits in the middle of "Hague Lake," named after Henry and Lydia Hague, who settled along the nearby lagoon in 1890. The lagoon was known by the original Salish inhabitants as *Clytosin*, meaning "water on both sides."

European settler culture often names places after themselves: Mount Denman, Earl's Cove, Port McNeill, whereas Indigenous cultures tend to name places after natural features. Likewise, Europeans tend to name the wild creatures after themselves—Cooper's hawk, MacGillivray's warbler, Dall's porpoise—whereas Indigenous cultures tend to name themselves after the creatures, or elements of nature—my friend Spotted Eagle, the famous Red Cloud, or Mistahimaskwa (Big Bear), the Plains Cree chief, who refused to sign a treaty in 1876 because he correctly suspected the discriminatory conditions would destroy his people's way of life and leave them in poverty.

The blue dasher appears motionless, as a statue. It rests on this rock island in a puddle, on an island in a lake, but this lake itself sits on an island that we call Cortes, named after the Spanish conquistador Hernán Cortés, who had nothing to do with this island, but who murdered his own wife, murdered thousands of Aztec people, stole their land, stole the silver and gold, and abducted men, women and children. Some islanders, over the years, have discussed changing this island's name from the mass-murdering colonizer Cortés to... what? There are Salish names for regions of the island, such as *Clytosin*, but no known name for the island itself. Fungi virtuoso Paul Stamets suggested Agarikon, after the famous medicinal mushrooms found here, high in old-growth fir trees. Someone else suggested Murrelet Island, after the seabirds who nest in the canopy of those ancient trees. Clytosin could apply to the entire island.

So the dragonfly sits on an island, in a puddle, on an island, in a lake, on an island, in the great Desolation Sound, so-named by British explorer George Vancouver, after his own sour mood, as he huddled in damp ship quarters, under the relentless rain, far from home, missing his wife and daughters. When the breeze swirls, the insect shudders, then calms and remains perfectly still again, eyes radiating the cool metallic colours. Why might we suspect that Captain Vancouver missed his daughters? He named nearby Mary Point on Cortes Island and Sarah Point, across Lewis Channel, after them.

The dragonfly swipes at his eyes. Like all insects, the blue dasher has six legs, but it cannot walk. The legs serve for grasping prey or perching, except for the two front legs, which have evolved into "eyebrushes," used for cleaning the surface of the compound eyes. Each eye facet contains light-sensitive opsin proteins. Humans possess three such proteins—for red, green and blue—but the day-flying dragonfly possesses five, one of which allows it to see ultraviolet (UV) light.

The thousands of facets produce a mosaic of images in the insect's brain, but how these impressions integrate into a picture of the world remains a mystery to curious humans. The upward-facing portion of the eye has only blue and UV receptors, composed by evolution's long progression, so that the flying predatory insect might clearly see prey insects against the bright sky. The downward-facing facets accept the longer wavelengths, the forest greens, orange and the browns of branches and stones. The dragonfly, like the rest of us, sees what it needs to see.

Ancestors of this blue dasher, the earliest arthropods, probably arose from ancient segmented worms some 800 million years ago, survived several small extinction events and emerged about 520 million years ago, as trilobites. Trilobites disappeared in the Devonian extinction, 340 million years ago, but some varieties evolved into marine eurypterids, the ancestors of all spiders, crustaceans and insects, such as our blue dasher.

Giant dragonflies, Meganeura, appeared about 325 million years ago, with a wingspan the size of a modern sharp-shinned hawk. These behemoth insects disappeared in the Great Permian Extinction, 250 million years ago, as Earth heated up and ninety-five percent of all species disappeared, the greatest biological holocaust of all time. However, their smaller relatives evolved into some 3,000 species of dragonfly that now live in every region of the world, all with a common ancestor, except for the unique Corduliidae family that includes the emerald dragonflies. The brown hawker, with distinctive bronze wings and turquoise dots along its brown body, was described and named in 1758 by Swedish naturalist Linnaeus, who invented modern biological classification. There is an organic farm named after him, Linnaea, on Cortes Island.

The name "Cortes" for this island in the northern Salish Sea appears as an accident of history and hubris. Captain Vancouver sailed here at the end of the eighteenth century to claim territory for England's King George III, who had just lost a war to the upstart American revolutionaries and would later wither away in bipolar delirium.

England and Spain remained at war when Vancouver first entered the inlet that he named after his friend Harry Burrard, although Spanish Captain José Narváez had already claimed the inlet for Spain and had mapped most of the Salish Sea. In spite of official conflict, Spanish commander Juan Francisco Bodega y Quadra graciously shared his maps with Vancouver. The two captains agreed to name the large island "Quadra and Vancouver Island," to commemorate their friendship. The British admiralty would have none of it, entered the simpler "Vancouver Island" on all maps, but agreed to toss off a few smaller islands to appease the Spanish.

Thus the Salish Sea remains dotted with islands such as Galiano, San Juan and Valdez. At the north end sits Quadra Island, after the Spanish captain; Hernando and Cortes, after the conquistador; and Marina, after one of Cortés's slave mistresses.

In 1519, Cortés departed Vera Cruz with 600 soldiers, horsemen, cannons and hundreds of enslaved Indigenous carriers for an assault on the Aztec capital at Tenochtitlan. He met resistance at Xalapa, destroyed the village and took twenty young women as slaves, handing them out as concubines for his officers. Among these, La Malinche, or "Marina," became his favorite mistress and bore him a son, Martín. Thus, Marina Island off the southwest coast of Cortes.

Hernán Cortés de Monroy, born in Medellín, Spain, in 1485, reportedly a pale and sickly child, failed at his Latin and law studies. Spanish historian Francisco Gómara describes the privileged youth as ruthless and haughty. He heard of Columbus's voyage at age sixteen, and as a failure in Spain, he dreamt of finding riches and prestige in Nueva España.

Cortés arrived in Hispaniola at the age of nineteen, married Catalina Juárez, sister-in-law of local Governor Diego Velázquez, gaining local status. He joined the conquest of Cuba and took a special interest in amassing slaves. During his march to Tenochtitlan, to terrorize the Aztecs and his own Indigenous slaves, Cortés massacred thousands of unarmed citizens in the plaza at Cholula, burned the city and took more warrior-slaves and concubines. At Tenochtitlan, he killed Moctezuma, subdued the Aztecs, plundered gold and silver, took more slaves and concocted the story, in letters to Spanish King Charles, that the Aztecs considered him a god.

In 1522, at the age of thirty-seven, Cortés coveted higher social status and set out to marry Spanish noblewoman Doña Juana de Zúñiga. To do so, according to a 19th-century investigation in Mexico, he murdered his wife, Catalina. He married Juana and gained the noble designation "Don." By 1530, he owned thirty-four silver mines and 23,000 vassals.

Dominican historian Bartolomé de Las Casas accused Cortés of brutality toward the Indigenous population. Franciscan historian Bernardino de Sahagún considered Cortés vicious and ruthless. Mayor Alonso de Estrada exiled him from New Spain for allegedly poisoning public officials. After the independence of México, Indigenous groups proposed that his remains "be publicly burned in front of the statue of Cuauhtemoc," the last Aztec leader. Perhaps, someday, we'll find a more esteemed name for our island. Cortés himself is perhaps most appropriately commemorated as *Orbiculare cortezii*, the Mexican lizard.

The evening air turns cool over Hague Lake, and the light dims. The blue dasher has not moved. I have not seen any females nearby. Males will defend feeding and breeding territories, chasing away other males or other large insects. Aerial battles are common along the shorelines, as males signal ownership by flashing their colours and darting at intruders. Females possess red eyes and typically remain hidden among the cattails, tule or sedge grass, when not mating or laying eggs, with their gold and black and white stripes offering camouflage.

The male and female blue dashers mate in flight. They hang on, face each other, and curl their abdomens to transfer sperm, forming a gyrating heart in midair. Then, the male stands guard from a perch while the female flies low over quiet, shallow water, bobbing up and down, tapping the water and laying several hundred eggs on the surface.

The larval nymphs remain in freshwater for up to four years as voracious predators, eating other larvae, small fish and tadpoles. Their lower jaw has a large extension armed with hooks and barbs. They typically moult a dozen times before they transform into an adult. The mature nymph raises its head from the water at night, adapts to breathing air, climbs a reed, typically a cattail, anchors itself to the stem and begins to split apart from behind the head. As Alfred Tennyson described this scene, "An inner impulse rent the veil / Of his old husk." The adult dragonfly arches backwards from the larval skin, swallows air and spreads its new wings.

After years as a larva, the adult blue dasher will only live a few weeks with wings and glorious colours. During this time, it will find a mate if possible, mate and die. As cold-blooded creatures, they bask in the sun to warm their blood and dry their wings. When hunting, the blue dasher will perch, waiting for prey, then dart out to catch it. This particular blue dasher, however, has not moved, even as shadows have crept over the rock. Its abdomen is taking on the frosty blue of age, and the wings appear tattered and discoloured. He appears old. He had his moment in the living miracle and may not have the energy to fly. I stealthily slip away, clamber down the rocks to my canoe on the lakeshore and paddle for home in the dying light.

SUE WHEELER

LASQUETI ISLAND

BEHOLD THE WATERS OF THE BAY

how they shrug off the captain's gaze
at any oncoming weather
and let the tiny fishes pass beneath the dock.

Hear the soft aluminum murmur of main-masts, and the water,
the beautiful water, is here, it's gone,
a hundred pictures silking its surface—rocks, trees,
pilings, windows, dances of colour and light.

The landed passengers ripple and hurry,
they gleam in swift pattern,
hung by the boots among the tavern's quivering lamps.

MOONLIT NIGHT, JANUARY

Bootprints in snow
from the porch
to where the truck
had been parked.

Tire tracks turning east
not west, out of the driveway.

So few secrets on an island.

ABOUT THE AUTHORS

Taiaiake Alfred was born in Montréal and raised in the Kahnawá:ke Mohawk Territory. He was a university professor for 25 years before resigning his position to take up writing, community work, public speaking and activism full-time. He is the recipient of a Canada Research Chair, the Native American Journalists Association's award for best column writing, the Native American and Indigenous Studies Association's award for one of the decade's most influential books and a National Aboriginal Achievement Award. He lives in the territory of the WSÁNEĆ Nation and is the father of three sons, all members of the Wet'suwet'en Nation.

Chris Arnett is an archaeologist/anthropologist/historian/author/musician/painter/carver who has lived on Salt Spring Island with his family for 30 years. A fourth-generation Vancouverite, he first visited Salt Spring as a teenager in the early 70s, camping all over the island with two friends. Interested in the history of the islands, Chris is the author of *The Terror of the Coast: Land Alienation and Colonial War on the Gulf Islands and Vancouver Island 1849-1863* and editor of *Two Houses Half-buried in Sand: Oral Traditions of the Hul'q'umi'num' Coast Salish of Kuper Island and Vancouver Island* by Beryl M. Cryer, both by Talonbooks.

Brenda Brooks still has a thing for Salt Spring Island—20 years and counting: hiking, kayaking, swimming, writing, café-hopping, laughing, crying. Over the years, she tapped into personal abilities she didn't know about until the island claimed her: dishwasher, cleaner, housekeeper, gardener, upholsterer. The things she did to hang onto that relationship! So many ultimatums—but did she leave? Some find Mt. Maxwell the height of sexiness (it's awesome!). But the view from Fernwood dock gets her every time. She has written two poetry collections and a novel. Her second novel, *HONEY*, will be published by ECW Press in the fall of 2019.

Maria Coffey, born and raised in England, came to British Columbia in 1985 and has lived here ever since, on Protection Island, Lasqueti Island and now Vancouver Island. Without previous experience or training as a writer, on Protection she penned her first book, *Fragile Edge*, now considered a classic in mountain literature. She went on to write eleven more books, winning prizes in Canada, the U.S. and Italy. With her husband, Dag Goering, she founded Hidden Places, an adventure travel company with a branch that advocates and fundraises for the welfare and conservation of elephants and other endangered species. www.hiddenplaces.net

Daniel Cowper was raised in a cabin built by his great-grandparents on Bowen Island. After studying in New York and Toronto, Daniel moved back to Bowen Island, where he built a cabin for his wife, the poet Emily Osborne, and their child. Daniel's poetry has appeared in Canadian, American and Irish literary reviews, including *Arc Poetry, Vallum* and *Southword*. *The God of Doors* was published in 2017 as co-winner of the Frog Hollow Press chapbook contest, and his first full-length collection, *Grotesque Tenderness*, was published by McGill-Queen's University Press.

William Deverell's first legal thriller, *Needles*, won the $50,000 Seal First Novel Prize. His subsequent nineteen novels and one non-fiction work include *Trial of Passion*, which won the Dashiell Hammett Award for literary excellence in crime writing in North America, and *April Fool*, which earned him his second Arthur Ellis Award for best Canadian crime novel. He created the CBC-TV drama *Street Legal*, newly revived in 2019. He holds honorary DLitt degrees from SFU and University of Saskatchewan. He shares a life, a home, and a half-acre organic garden, on Pender Island, with his wife, biologist Jan Kirkby. His life and works can be viewed at www.deverell.com

Ann Eriksson, author and biologist, has lived, worked and played in the Gulf Islands for over forty years. She is the author of five novels and a non-fiction book for children about ocean conservation. Passionate about the environment, Ann is the Gulf Island Region technical coordinator for the Salish Sea Nearshore Habitat Recovery Project, an initiative to restore eelgrass and shoreline ecosystems in the Salish Sea. A founding director of the Thetis Island Nature Conservancy, Ann lives on Thetis Island with her husband, poet Gary Geddes. www.annaeriksson.ca.

Mona Fertig loves islands. She is a poet, book artist, editor and publisher at Mother Tongue Publishing, home of the Unheralded Artists of BC series. She started Canada's first literary center, the Literary Storefront, in Vancouver, which operated from 1978 to 1985. The VPL made her a Literary Landmark in 2016. Fertig has been the B.C. Rep for PEN Canada and TWUC. Her books include *Sex, Death & Travel, The Unsettled* and *The Life and Art of George Fertig,* and she is working on a new poetry collection. In 1990 she moved to Salt Spring Island with her husband, Peter Haase, and their son and daughter.

Cathy Ford has had a passionate domestic relationship with Mayne Island for more than four decades. Often described as "the witch flying on a broom," its beauty, landscape, history, secrets and stories have informed all her work. She earned a BFA and MFA, both with honours, from UBC. Married, with one son birthed on Mayne Island, the only child born on-island in a half century. Long-term member of LCP and TWUC, she has published many books of poetry and long poems, including *the art of breathing underwater* and *Flowers We Will Never Know the Names Of,* both with Mother Tongue Publishing.

Gary Geddes has written and edited fifty books of poetry, fiction, drama, non-fiction, criticism, translation and anthologies and won a dozen national and international literary awards, including the Commonwealth Poetry Prize (Americas Region), the Lieutenant Governor's Award for Literary Excellence and the Gabriela Mistral Prize from the government of Chile. His non-fiction works include *Drink the Bitter Root* and *Medicine Unbundled: A Journey Through the Minefields of Indigenous Health Care.* His most recent books of poetry are *What Does a House Want?* and *The Resumption of Play.* He lives on Thetis Island with his wife, the novelist Ann Eriksson.

Katherine Palmer Gordon moved to Gabriola Island in 2003 to find time, space and inspiration to write. There has been no shortage of the latter. She is now the author of six award-winning books about British Columbia and has published numerous articles and essays in both Canada and New Zealand, her other home. She has two more books in progress. In her spare time, she negotiates treaties.

Peter Haase was born in Liverpool, England, and immigrated to Australia at age seventeen and later to Canada. Throughout his travels, he's been an electrician/builder, singer/entertainer, letterpress printer/linocut artist, scripture teacher, writer, gardener, commercial fisher and has sport fished from the Yukon to Australia. An environmental/political activist, Haase believes in clean energy. He wrote an early memoir, *Liverpool Lad: Adventures Growing Up in Postwar Liverpool* (Mother Tongue Publishing) and is currently working on his second book, *Double Immigrant.* He lives with his wife, Mona Fertig, on Salt Spring Island, and still loves to fish.

Amanda Hale has lived on Hornby Island for thirty years, painting, sculpting and writing in many genres. She has published three novels, two collections of linked fictions set in the Cuban town of Baracoa and two poetry chapbooks. She won the Prism International Prize for Creative Non-fiction, and has twice been a finalist for the ReLit Fiction Award. Amanda is the librettist for an original opera, *Pomegranate,* set in ancient Pompei, to premiere in Toronto, summer of 2019. Her novel *Mad Hatter* will be published in the fall of 2019 by Guernica Editions.

Diana Hayes has lived on the east and west coasts of Canada. She studied at UBC and UVic, receiving a BA and MFA in creative writing. She has published six books, including *This Is the Moon's Work: New and Selected Poems.* Her recent poetry was included in the anthologies *Rocksalt, Force Field* and *111 West Coast Literary Portraits,* all with Mother Tongue Publishing. Her new book of poems, *Labyrinth of Green* will be published by Plumleaf Press in fall 2019. Her practice of year-round ocean swimming inspired the formation of the Salt Spring Seals in 2002. Salt Spring Island has been home since 1981.

Jack Hodgins' novels and story collections include *Spit Delaney's Island, The Invention of the World, Innocent Cities, Broken Ground* and *Damage Done by the Storm. A Passion for Narrative* (a guide to writing fiction) is used in classrooms and writing groups in Canada and Australia. He has won the Governor General's Award, the Canada–Australia Prize and the Ethel Wilson Fiction Prize, among others. In 2006 he was awarded both the Terasen Lifetime Achievement Award and the Lieutenant Governor's Award for Literary

Excellence in British Columbia. In 2010 he was appointed a Member of the Order of Canada. He and his wife, Dianne, live in Victoria. www.jackhodgins.ca

In **Cornelia Hoogland's** seven books, she locates her metaphors in Canada's West Coast landscape and concerns. An expert in the fairy tale "Little Red Riding Hood," Cornelia wrote a full-length play, *RED,* and poetry, *Woods Wolf Girl* (shortlisted for the ReLit Award for Poetry), as well as fiction and memoir that explore the profound impact of fairy-tale imagery. Her latest book, *Trailer Park Elegy*, was a finalist for the League of Canadian Poets 2018 Raymond Souster Award. She was recently shortlisted for the CBC Literary Prize in Poetry and in Nonfiction. Cornelia lives and writes on Hornby Island. www. corneliahoogland.com

Stephen Hume came to the Salish Sea more than 70 years ago. He and his wife bought land on Saturna Island over 40 years ago, built a house and lived there in the early 1990s. He now lives near T̲EUWEN̲ on the end of the Saanich Peninsula overlooking Satellite Channel. Hume has written twelve books of poetry, essays, natural history, history and biography. His most recent is *A Walk with the Rainy Sisters*, Harbour Publishing.

Christina Johnson-Dean has been going to Gambier Island since 1985. She has written three books for Mother Tongue Publishing's Unheralded Artists of BC series on artists Ina D.D. Uhthoff (finalist for the City of Victoria Butler Book Prize), Edythe Hembroff-Schleicher and Mary Filer. Originally from Berkeley, California (where she graduated from UCB in history and art), she completed an MA in History in Art at the University of Victoria, resulting in the B.C. Archives publication *The Crease Family: A Record of Settlement and Service in British Columbia.* She resides in Victoria with her husband; they have two daughters and two grandchildren.

Des Kennedy is a novelist and essayist as well as a veteran back-to-the-lander and political activist. He's the author of ten books, including four novels, a memoir and five works of creative non-fiction about gardening and rural living. Three of his titles were shortlisted for the Stephen Leacock Memorial Medal for

Humour. His latest book is a novel titled *Beautiful Communions*, by Ronsdale Press, 2018, and he is currently at work on a new novel. Des and his partner, Sandy, live a conserver lifestyle in their hand-built house surrounded by gardens and woodlands on Denman Island.

Michael Kenyon was born in Sale, England, and has lived on the West Coast since 1967. A seaman with the Coast Guard, he first set foot on Pender Island at Port Washington in 1971 and the following year bought a cottage on Port Washington Road. The island population then was 500 and now is 2,500. Pender has been the quiet retreat, the listening home, place of magic, ever since, and the mainstay of his psychotherapeutic practice for fifteen years. Almost every major writing project and relationship has had incubation time there. His recent collection of poetry is *Lamb,* with Pedlar Press, 2018.

Zoë Landale has published seven books, edited two books, and contributed to over forty anthologies. Her writing has won significant awards in three genres, including the Stony Brook $1000 Short Fiction Prize, National Magazine Gold for memoir and the CBC Poetry Prize. For fifteen years, she was a faculty member in the Creative Writing Department at Kwantlen Polytechnic University in Vancouver. She lives on Pender Island where she is a crew member of the volunteer search and rescue boat. Zoë's eighth book of poetry is forthcoming with Inanna Publications.

Peter Levitt has published seventeen books of poetry and prose, including translations from Chinese, Japanese and Spanish. Legendary poet Robert Creeley wrote that Peter's writing "sounds the honour of our common dance," and in 1989 Peter received the Lannan Foundation Literary Award in Poetry. He is the associate and translation editor of the Zen classic, *Treasury of the True Dharma Eye: Zen Master Dogen's Shobo Genzo*, and has translated and edited other Zen books, including work by Thich Nhat Hanh. He lives with his wife, poet Shirley Graham, and their son, on Salt Spring Island where he is the guiding teacher of the Salt Spring Zen Circle.

Derek Lundy is the author of five books: *Scott Turow: Meeting the Enemy; Godforsaken Sea: Racing the World's Most Dangerous Waters*; *The Way of a Ship: A Square-Rigger Voyage in the Last Days of Sail*; *The Bloody Red Hand: A Journey Through Truth, Myth and Terror in Northern Ireland* and *Borderlands: Riding the Edge of America*. He lives on Salt Spring Island where some of his family first settled in the late 1880s.

Matsuki Masutani moved from Tokyo to Vancouver in 1976. Ten years later, he moved to Denman Island, where he eventually began writing poems in English and Japanese. These poems have only been shared with friends and family until recently. Matsuki is a freelance translator and has translated Canadian works such as Roy Kiyooka's *Mothertalk*, Hiromi Goto's *Chorus of Mushroom* and Alice Munro's *Who Do You Think You Are* (in process).

Karen McLaughlin grew up in Nova Scotia and lived in seven provinces before settling on Thetis Island for eighteen years. In 2015 she moved to Victoria. Karen graduated from the Alberta College of Art in 1991. She has shown her work and read from her novels in municipal galleries and artist-run centres across Canada. Karen is currently a senior resident at the Vancouver Island School of Art where she also teaches art reading and writing. Although she still gets homesick for Thetis Island, she can often be spotted flying along Dallas Road and Beach Drive on her electric bicycle.

Maureen Moore is the author of three published novels. *The Illumination of Alice Mallory* was shortlisted for the Ethel Wilson Fiction Prize. She's received several awards for her volunteer work—Islands Trust Environmental Stewardship Award, Salt Spring Island Conservancy Volunteer of the year 2008, Land Trust Alliance Conservation Award—and she's recognized as a Bioneer Change-Maker. She lives on Salt Spring Island.

Arleen Paré has been living part-time on Mayne Island since 1984. She and her wife own a house at David Cove, where she spends time watching the water and the myriad birds that harbour there. She has written five books, mainly collections of poetry, has been a finalist for the Dorothy Livesay Poetry Prize and has won a City of Victoria Butler Book Prize, a CBC Bookie Award, an American Golden Crown Literary Award and the Governor General's Award for Poetry. She lives in Victoria.

Briony Penn grew up on a 300-million-year-old Wrangellian island in the Salish Sea. Her great-great-grandmother brought holly, ivy, broom and gorse to the unceded territory of Saanich families at WENNANEC. The sins of her ancestors are visited daily. She wishes more drivers would watch out for snakes in the summer and frogs/newts in the fall. Her book *The Real Thing: The Natural History of Ian McTaggart Cowan* won a 2016 Roderick Haig-Brown Non-Fiction Prize. Recent releases include an updated *Year on the Wild Side* and collaborations with Xenaksiala elder Cecil Paul, in *Stories from the Magic Canoe of Wa'xaid* and *Following the Good River*.

Michael Redican has lived on Quadra Island for twenty years. He spends his days gardening, teaching bridge, noodling on the piano and writing. His most recent book is *Streets of New York* (*Bridge Poems for Bridge Players*).

Murray Reiss is an award-winning poet whose first book, *The Survival Rate of Butterflies in the Wild,* won the 2014 Gerald Lampert Memorial Award. He has lived on Salt Spring Island since the summer of 1979, having arrived (with his wife, Karen, and daughter, Kaya) purely by ferry-line accident. He's lived in the north end, on Duck Creek, and the south end, on Stowell Creek, and can imagine living nowhere else on Earth. He brings his words to life on the stage as well as the page as a climate action performance poet and founding member of Salt Spring's Only Planet Cabaret.

Linda Rogers doesn't know of an island in the Salish Sea she can't rhyme with, beginning with Savary where she spent the happiest days of her childhood listening to saltwater and cedars, the best kind of music. She is a novelist, poet, essayist, editor and songwriter, author of twenty-nine books, past Victoria Poet Laureate and President of the League of Canadian Poets. Her most recent books are *Crow Jazz* with Mother Tongue Publishing and *Hi! Wik'sas* with Kwakwaka'wakw artist Chief Rande Cook, Exile Editions.

Christine Smart writes poetry and fiction. *The White Crow* is her latest collection of poetry, published in 2013 by Hedgerow Press. Her first book, *Decked and Dancing*, won the Acorn-Plantos Award for Peoples Poetry in 2007. Since 1989, she has lived on Salt Spring Island where she gardens, sails, swims and hikes. Chris is the artistic director for the Salt Spring Poetry Open Mic series. www.christinesmart.ca/

Gail Sjuberg lives on Salt Spring Island and is the long-time editor of the award-winning *Gulf Islands Driftwood* newspaper, *Aqua* magazine and other publications. Gail intended to become a professional accordion player until a passion for Canadian literature, history and politics led her to earn a BA in Canadian Studies at Simon Fraser University instead. She chaired the Salt Spring Literacy Society from 2013 to 2019, is an avid Nia dancer and can occasionally still be heard playing the accordion as part of The Last Schmaltz group.

Steven Ross Smith, over three decades, has visited and lived part-time in a cabin on five acres on Galiano Island. Five years ago, he purchased a kayak to get to know, more intimately, the waters around the island, and to write about the experiences. Over those same decades, he's crafted a multi-book poetic series called *fluttertongue*, now six books long. Even when on Galiano, he carries the honour of being the 2019 Banff Poet Laureate. His work has won awards and appears in print, audio and video in Canada, U.S. and abroad. He's known for his expressive work, which gives close attention to language's sonority.

George Szanto is the author of nearly two dozen books, including his Mexico trilogy—*The Underside of Stones, Second Sight, The Condesa of M.*—his recent *Whatever Lola Wants* and a chronicle/memoir, *Bog Tender*. His first novel, *Not Working*, was cited by *Books in Canada* as one of the five best first novels of 1982. *Friends & Marriages* won the Hugh MacLennan Prize for Fiction for 1995. With his co-writer Sandy Frances Duncan, he has written an islands detective series, including *Never Sleep with a Suspect on Gabriola Island* and *Always Kiss the Corpse on Whidbey Island*. He lives on Gabriola Island. georgeszanto.com

Nancy J. Turner, distinguished professor emerita in Environmental Studies, University of Victoria, has worked with elders and cultural specialists in western Canada for over fifty years, helping to document Indigenous knowledge of plants and environments. She has authored, co-authored or co-edited over twenty books (including *Plants of Haida Gwaii, The Earth's Blanket, Keeping It Living* and *Saanich Ethnobotany*) and over 140 book chapters and papers. Her book *Ancient Pathways, Ancestral Knowledge* received the Canada Prize for Social Sciences. Other awards include Order of British Columbia (1999), Order of Canada (2009) and honorary degrees from VIU, UBC, UNBC and SFU. She and her husband, Bob, have enjoyed life on Protection Island for ten years.

M.C. Warrior, an immigrant from the U.K., spent some thirty-five years at what was once the sharp end of production on the B.C. coast, first logging and then commercial fishing. Most years he would fish herring in March around Hornby and Denman and then salmon in August around Sabine Pass, between Lasqueti and Texada. Warrior later lived briefly on Lasqueti and now lives on Gabriola, five minutes' walk from Lock Bay. His book of poetry, *Disappearing Minglewood Blues,* will be published by Mother Tongue in 2020.

Alison Watt is an artist and writer who has lived on Protection Island for over twenty years. As a young biologist, she studied puffins on the remote Triangle Island and has worked as a naturalist each summer for over twenty years on another seabird colony, Mitlenatch Island in the northern Salish Sea. Her first book, *The Last Island: A Naturalist's Sojourn on Triangle Island*, won the Edna Staebler Award for Creative Non-fiction. Other books include *Circadia* (Pedlar Press), and a novel, *Dazzle Patterns* (Freehand Books), was nominated for the 2018 Amazon Canada First Novel Award.

Bob Weeden went West in 1955, after a youth spent in New England. He moved to Alaska in 1959 with bride Judy and a PhD in zoology from UBC. After leading bird studies for a decade with the Alaska Department of Fish and Game, he taught natural resources management at UA (Fairbanks). Retiring in 1990 to Salt Spring Island, Judy gardens and pots while Bob tends a small farm and reads and writes. He delights in learning about the world and for sixty years has helped take care of it through conservation volunteering.

Rex Weyler is a writer and ecologist. His books include *Blood of the Land: A History of Indigenous American Nations*, nominated for a Pulitzer Prize; *Greenpeace: The Inside Story*, a finalist for the Shaughnessy Cohen Prize for Political Writing; and *The Jesus Sayings: The Quest for His Authentic Message*, a deconstruction of first-century history and finalist for the Hubert Evans Non-Fiction Prize. In the 1970s, Rex was a co-founder of Greenpeace International and editor of the *Greenpeace Chronicles*, the organization's newsletter. He currently posts the "Deep Green" column on Greenpeace International's website. He lives on Cortes Island with his wife, artist Lisa Gibbons.

Sue Wheeler has published three collections of poetry: *Solstice on the Anacortes Ferry* (Kalamalka Press), winner of the Kalamalka New Writers Prize; *Slow-Moving Target* (Brick Books), shortlisted for the Dorothy Livesay Poetry Prize and the Pat Lowther Memorial Award; and *Habitat* (Brick Books). She has lived for over forty years on a seaside farm on Lasqueti Island.

ABOUT THE ARTIST AND HER PAINTINGS

Nicola Wheston was born in London in 1953, immigrated to Canada in 1976 and became a citizen in 1986. She studied at the Ruskin School of Drawing at Oxford University and the Nova Scotia School of Art and Design. Her paintings have been in group and solo shows and are in collections in Mexico, North America and the UK. Nicola is primarily a figurative painter, but since living on Salt Spring, she has also created landscapes of the Salish Sea, through which she has come to know the islands, the seasonal cycles and the environmental impact by humanity. www.nicolawheston.com

Front Cover: *Southey Point*, 2005, oil on canvas.

1. *August Twin Oaks*, 2002, oil on canvas, page 41
2. *Maple in Sunlight*, 2010, oil on canvas, page 47
3. *Blackburn Lake*, 2013, oil on canvas, page 65
4. *Port Renfrew Tides*, 2013, oil on canvas, page 85
5. *Root*, 2007, oil on canvas, page 101
6. *Malcolm Island*, 2006, oil on canvas, page 113-114
7. *Stormy Sky Branches*, 2009, oil on canvas, page 129
8. *Ruckle Park*, Stormy Tree, 2009, oil on canvas, page 140
9. *Sunlight Douglas-fir*, 2013, oil on canvas, page 151
10. *Summer Arbutus II*, 2012, oil on canvas, page 173
11. *Twin Oaks End of Summer*, 2007, oil on canvas, page 187

Back Cover: *Winter Twin Oaks*, 2002, oil on canvas.

Photography by David Borrowman